Impact of Public-Private P

Ignatius Mugabo

Impact of Public-Private Partnership on Community Development

A Case Study of Education Sector 1994-2008: Rwanda

LAP LAMBERT Academic Publishing

Impressum/Imprint (nur für Deutschland/ only for Germany)
Bibliografische Information der Deutschen Nationalbibliothek: Die Deutsche Nationalbibliothek verzeichnet diese Publikation in der Deutschen Nationalbibliografie; detaillierte bibliografische Daten sind im Internet über http://dnb.d-nb.de abrufbar.

Alle in diesem Buch genannten Marken und Produktnamen unterliegen warenzeichen-, marken- oder patentrechtlichem Schutz bzw. sind Warenzeichen oder eingetragene Warenzeichen der jeweiligen Inhaber. Die Wiedergabe von Marken, Produktnamen, Gebrauchsnamen, Handelsnamen, Warenbezeichnungen u.s.w. in diesem Werk berechtigt auch ohne besondere Kennzeichnung nicht zu der Annahme, dass solche Namen im Sinne der Warenzeichen- und Markenschutzgesetzgebung als frei zu betrachten wären und daher von jedermann benutzt werden dürften.

Coverbild: www.ingimage.com

Verlag: LAP LAMBERT Academic Publishing GmbH & Co. KG
Dudweiler Landstr. 99, 66123 Saarbrücken, Deutschland
Telefon +49 681 3720-310, Telefax +49 681 3720-3109
Email: info@lap-publishing.com

Herstellung in Deutschland:
Schaltungsdienst Lange o.H.G., Berlin
Books on Demand GmbH, Norderstedt
Reha GmbH, Saarbrücken
Amazon Distribution GmbH, Leipzig
ISBN: 978-3-8443-0017-8

Imprint (only for USA, GB)
Bibliographic information published by the Deutsche Nationalbibliothek: The Deutsche Nationalbibliothek lists this publication in the Deutsche Nationalbibliografie; detailed bibliographic data are available in the Internet at http://dnb.d-nb.de.

Any brand names and product names mentioned in this book are subject to trademark, brand or patent protection and are trademarks or registered trademarks of their respective holders. The use of brand names, product names, common names, trade names, product descriptions etc. even without a particular marking in this works is in no way to be construed to mean that such names may be regarded as unrestricted in respect of trademark and brand protection legislation and could thus be used by anyone.

Cover image: www.ingimage.com

Publisher: LAP LAMBERT Academic Publishing GmbH & Co. KG
Dudweiler Landstr. 99, 66123 Saarbrücken, Germany
Phone +49 681 3720-310, Fax +49 681 3720-3109
Email: info@lap-publishing.com

Printed in the U.S.A.
Printed in the U.K. by (see last page)
ISBN: 978-3-8443-0017-8

Copyright © 2011 by the author and LAP LAMBERT Academic Publishing GmbH & Co. KG and licensors
All rights reserved. Saarbrücken 2011

What impact has Public-Private Partnership had on Community Development in Rwanda?

A Case Study of Education Sector 1994-2008

By Ignatius Mugabo

....

Table of Contents

1. Dedication   3
2. Acknowledgement   3
3. Foreword   5
4. Chapter One: Introduction to the Study   7
   - ❖ Background to this Study.. 7
   - ❖ Introduction to Rwanda... 8
   - ❖ Research Aims and Objectives.. 13
   - ❖ The Significance of the Study.. 14
   - ❖ The Research Structure... 15
5. Chapter Two: Literature Review   17
   - ❖ Introduction.. 17
   - ❖ Definition of PPP.. 19
   - ❖ A Brief History of PPP... 24
   - ❖ Advantages, Spectrum and Models of PPP............................. 28
   - ❖ Weaknesses and Limitations... 37

- ❖ Keys to Success or Failure of PPP..........39
- ❖ Community Development..........42
- ❖ Community Development vs. Economic Growth..........45
- ❖ PPP vs. Community Development..........50
- ❖ Lessons for Rwanda..........52

6. **Chapter Three: Research Methodology** — 59
   - ❖ The choice of research methodology..........59
   - ❖ Data collection..........62
   - ❖ Data validation and administration..........63
   - ❖ Ethical Considerations..........65

7. **Chapter Four: Analysis and Case Studies** — 69
   - ❖ Data Analysis Approach..........69
   - ❖ A Brief Overview of PPP in Rwanda..........70
   - ❖ PPP Framework in Rwanda..........73
   - ❖ PPP Case Studies in Rwanda's education sector..........77
   - ❖ Case Study 1: Kigali Institute of Science and Technology..........80
   - ❖ Case Study2: One Laptop per Child..........83

   - ❖ Conclusion..........85

8. **Chapter Five: Conclusion** — 86

9. Chapter Six: References & Appendices   91

   ❖ **Appendix A**: *Explanatory Statement and Consent Form*

   ❖ **Appendix B**: *Former Military College, now KIST*

   ❖ **Appendix C**: Abbreviations and Acronyms

i. **Dedication**

Dedicated to my family for their love, support and prayers during this course and always.

ii. **Acknowledgement**

I am very grateful to all my lecturers at London Metropolitan University's Department of Applied Social Sciences (DASS), especially course leader John Eversley, who became my dissertation supervisor. His vast experience and knowledge of community and voluntary sector management and public policy helped shape my understanding of dilemmas and contradictions of policy making in both the public and voluntary sectors. I am equally grateful to Dr Ezendu Ariwa of London Metropolitan Business School (LMBS), who co-supervised this dissertation. His wide experience and knowledge of business and communications strategy provided the link I was looking for, between business, community development and social change.

My managers at the London Fire and Emergency Planning Authority/ London Fire Brigade (LFEPA/LFB), thank you for your support, which enabled me to combine this course with my work. To all my friends who encouraged me to toughen up whenever the going got tough, thank you. Special thanks to Dr Tamara Dragadze, who was very helpful at the time I needed her professional advice most.

I wish to reserve the sweetest words and thanks to my wife Jackie, who stood with and supported me from start to finish, and my boys William and Gideon who missed our routine evening activities, as I concentrated on this research. Without mentioning each of them, my immense gratitude goes to the Rwandan officials, at the Embassy of Rwanda in London, the Ministries of Finance, commerce and local government; Rwanda Development Board, Rwanda Economic and Social Council, and Kigali Institute of Science and Technology. This project would not have been successful without your support and responses to my enquiry. For any errors, omissions, I take full responsibility.

iii. FOREWORD

This dissertation project examines the Public-Private Partnership (PPP) and community development policies and practice in Rwanda. The main research questions are: What is the shape of PPP in Rwanda? What systems, policies and other supportive 'soft' infrastructure are in place to ensure the country benefits from PPP? What consideration, if any, does the PPP policy in Rwanda give to community development? What contribution could it make to community development? What is the relationship between community development and economic growth?

This research is based on a literature review and analysis of relevant policy documents and academic literature, taking some PPP case studies from Rwanda's education sector, but efforts were also made to solicit the views of Rwandan officials who have been involved in development of PPP or other related polices since 1994. Given the practical difficulties of conducting research in Rwanda, correspondences with identified officials were by email and /or telephone.

The findings of this study show that PPP in Rwanda is still a young concept and largely not well understood, by both the public and private sectors, and that implementation mechanisms and policies on the ground are still lacking or very weak, although political backing is very strong. Findings further show that community development is often confused with economic development, and that PPP has not had any serious impact in this field. This study, however, notes that Rwanda is determined to build proper functioning PPP systems and there evidence they want to use it to achieve *social welfare* for the Rwandan people. The study concludes that the concept of community development needs to be distinguished from economic development/growth, and in addition to pursuing economic growth, PPP should and can be used to achieve community development as well.

CHAPTER ONE

1.0 INTRODUCTION TO THE STUDY

Background to this study

PPP is an area of public policy I first became interested in at a personal level, when my two sons were born in a magnificent modern hospital in London, University College London Hospital, constructed via one of PPP models, Private Finance Initiative (PFI). Public infrastructure projects like that one are known to be constructed by government money and, justifiably owned by the public, or the facility is private and people pay, normally dearly, to use it; at least that was my understanding. But here we have a public facility, used by the public under the National Health Service (NHS) yet it was apparently built by private money. It sounded to me like a contradiction in terms, though a very interesting one and I wanted to know how that could be possible. When these thoughts started disturbing my mind, up until when I embarked on this study, I did not know that in 1959 C. Wright Mills had advanced the reasoning that never separate work from life. In his book *The Sociological Imagination (1959)*, Mills added an appendix entitled 'On Intellectual Craftmanship' in which he asserted that ideas and insights from life can often provide the trigger or clue for theoretical understanding of the issues we are researching (cited in Fisher, 2007:8). Berg (2001) states that every research project starts from an idea, personal experiences or observations. It is during these hospital visits that my common sense understanding of how public services are provided was challenged and the foundation for this research was laid.

My interest in PPP and public policy increased when I started working in the British public service where various PPP models are widely used to deliver infrastructure and other public sector investment projects. When I enrolled at London Metropolitan I was introduced to the concept of 'community development' as opposed to 'economic development/growth'. Although I have been involved in community work for many years, I was not aware of community development as a profession or as an academic field of study.

In most literature on Public Private Partnership, economic growth/development is always cited as the reason for adopting the concept (Savas, 2006; Gosling, 2004; IPPR, 2001). Community development is rarely advanced as a reason for PPP, although some advocates seem to assume that it will follow economic growth (IPPR, 2001).

Whereas economic growth is about the growth of output per head (Lewis, 1976; Little, 1982), community development is about empowering local communities to take charge of their own destinies by getting involved in, and influencing activities, policies and decisions that affect them (Taylor *et al,* 2000; Ledwith, 2005; Department for Communities and Local Government, 2007). This study is interested in how and if economic growth and community development can be pursued together; and whether PPP can be used to achieve both, not one at the expense of the other.

Introduction to Rwanda
Rwanda is a small, hilly and densely populated country in East Africa, 120 Kilometres south of the equator. The total land mass is 26,338 sq.km, of

which about 1400 sq.km is water. The Rwandan population is now approaching 10 million (CHRI, 2009) and about 90% live in rural areas. The former Belgian colony was devastated by the Genocide in 1994, in which about 1 million people of Tutsi minority were killed by extremist elements of the majority Hutu. The country has made a dramatic recovery and is now seen by some as possible development success story in Africa. In a 2008 report by Mo Ibrahim Foundation, Rwanda was assessed on five criteria of safety and security, rule of law, transparency and corruption, participation and human rights, sustainable economic development and human development, and found to be the 'most improved country in Africa', and similar sentiments were recently expressed in the Washington Post of the United States of America (Mo Ibrahim Index, 2008; Lacy, 2009). Several international commentators have cited Rwanda as the safest country in Africa (Amanpour, 2008; Adams, 2009), and some see post-genocide Rwanda as an experiment in social engineering (Stiem, 2009). (A further discussion of the history of Rwanda is available on the government internet website http://www.gov.rw)

To sustain the progress already registered, PPP has been identified by the Rwandan government as a quick route to infrastructure development, which will in turn support rapid economic growth (Musoni, 2008; Bihire, 2009). The government wants to use PPP to improve the quality of public services and attract private sector money into public sector investments, according to the National Public Investment Policy (NPIP, 2009).

It is argued that PPP offers a better way of attracting private sector money, skills and efficiency into public investment projects, and allows the sharing of risks and responsibility with private firms (Joseph & Kelly, eds., 2000). Experts credit PPP for avoiding the pitfalls of full privatization such as mass lay-off of public sector workers and inflated prices for goods and services, while allowing government to retain control and ownership of public infrastructure (Farlam, 2005). Private firms can provide the services traditionally a preserve of the public sector, efficiently and at less cost, resulting in better value for money for the taxpayer (Gosling, 2004).

Experts also say PPP is used by "financially strained municipalities to reform their operations" (Collin & Hanson, in Osborne, 2000:204).

But like privatization, PPP is also prone to political influence, mismanagement and corruption (Gosling, 2004).

Although Rwanda has embarked on fighting corruption with vigour that is not seen in neighbouring countries, corruption is still being reported in the public sector, especially in the judiciary, police and tender management (Musoni, Kagire, 2009). Corruption and shoddy work practices also continue to be reported in the construction and other public works (Mutara, 2009).

For a country to reap the benefits of PPP there is a need for political commitment from the top, a highly disciplined and qualified PPP team and participation from both public and private sectors. Governments also need to improve the way they work with the private sector and put in place high standard, transparent procedures and a regulatory framework (Gosling, 2004; OECD, 2008).

Rwanda still lacks the regulatory and legislative framework to support this very complex initiative. Worse still, there is an acute lack of human capacity in the public sector to prepare and negotiate good PPP projects for the country (Kagame, 2009).

There is also a deficit of policy debate within the public and private sectors on PPP. A communication specialist from the country's private sector organisation (PSF) tried to provoke this debate and was fired instantly (Kakimba, 2009; The New Times editorial, 2009), which is an indication that the private sector shares the blame for the lack of policy debates. While political backing is very important for the success of PPP in any country (Hamilton, 2008; UNDP, 2004), an informed debate is also crucial (Davie, 2008), as debate informs policy making and attracts public and private sector buy-in.

Critics say that is typical of the current Rwandan government; too ambitious, sets unachievable targets for a developing, impoverished country and does not allow room for debating policies (Kinzer, 2008, The Economist Magazine, 2008, CNN, 2009). President Paul Kagame, the force behind the country's ambitions, wants his country to achieve middle income status by 2020 and is unapologetic for aiming higher (Vision 2020). He believes that you would rather aim higher and miss some of your targets than aiming lower and hit all your targets (Kagame, *address to Rwandan community in London,* 2006).

Critics also argue that Paul Kagame's government is pursuing an aggressive economic development agenda at the expense of the poor and has little regard for political, press freedoms and human rights (CHRI, 2009). Yet the Rwandan government argues that to give full rights and freedoms to a hungry and ignorant population in a country with no strong institutions to sustain and defend the freedoms, is meaningless as they will be manipulated by the elite and could take the country back to violence (Kagame's speech at National University of Singapore, 2008; and interview on CNN, 2009). There is evidence that Rwanda's history backs the government's line of thinking.

Informed, therefore, by its history Rwanda has adopted a "consensual" political dispensation (Kayumba, 2008), where all political parties are asked to come to an agreement on a common agenda for the country, and work together to achieve it (Gatete, *address to the Rwandan community in London*, 2009). The current agenda is called "Vision 2020", which aims to make Rwanda a middle- income country by the year 2020 (MINECOFIN, 2007). The consensus building policy also underlies the creation of the Inter-Party Forum, the Joint Development Forum and the Public Private Partnerships, which bring together the government, opposition parties, the business community and the civil society (RESC, 2009). Rwanda Economic and Social Council (RESC) is the coordinating agency of the consensus building model in Rwanda[1]. Rwanda is not the first country to adopt PPP as it has been used as a procurement method in developed countries for decades, and is increasingly becoming an important concept in infrastructure development in many developing countries, but it is also controversial (Gosling, 2004).

---

[1] *Presidential Order N° 64/01 dated 31/12/2007*

Proponents say that unlike extremes like 'pure public ownership' or 'pure private ownership', PPP uniquely marries well the interests of both the public and private sectors, and allegedly saves taxpayers' money through efficient management of resources associated with the private sector (Ghobadian, et al, 2004). They believe the public sector is "inimical to the enterprise culture" (Morgan & Roberts, 1993:6) and therefore cannot deliver efficient management of resources as the private sector does. Yet opponents argue that PPP is privatization by stealth, undermines the ethos of public service and the principles of social equity (Ghobadian *et al.*, 2004) and that the taxpayer pays more in the long run (Gosling, 2004).They also argue that the private entity enters PPP primarily to make a return on investment at the expense of taxpayers, and if the public interest in PPP is not well defined and defended, the public sector partner may give up more than it receives, hence losing out to the private sector partners (GOA, 2008).

Research Aims and Objectives

This study aims to examine pertinent issues in PPP from an economic standpoint, taking some case studies from Rwanda's education sector. The specific objectives and questions to be answered include:

What is the definition and history of PPP? What are its economic advantages? What factors contribute to its success or failure? What is the history and nature of PPP in Rwanda; and is there any supportive policies and infrastructure? What are the pull and/or push factors for PPP in Rwanda; and what factors are likely to affect its success?

The study also analyses PPP from another angle- a *community development* angle. Achieving *Economic development* drives most of development policy in many developing countries, including Rwanda (NPIP, 2009). PPP is seen as a quick route to critical infrastructure that will act as a backbone for rapid economic growth. How PPP can incorporate community development principles in its routine will be examined. The study strives to provide some insights into the shape of PPP in Rwanda, what it is intended to achieve, its relationship with economic growth/development and community development and how PPP can contribute to the achievement of both.

The Significance of the Study

This study will probably be the first study to look at PPP in Rwanda, and its relationship with economic growth and community development, and it could provide useful insights to key stakeholders in Rwanda and beyond. Findings of this study could stimulate further interest and curiosity among policy makers, students and scholars and could lead to further investigations of how PPP can be used not only to achieve economic growth, but community development as well.

Furthermore it could specifically offer insight into the way Rwanda implements its PPP policy for the overall benefit of the Rwandan people, not simply a few local entrepreneurs and Multinational Corporations.

The Research Structure

This study relies on literature review - a form of qualitative research methodology. It will review existing literature and analyse relevant policy documents and academic material, and seek the views of Rwandan officials and international organisations officials who have been involved in development/economic policy in Rwanda from 1994.

Chapter One gives a general introduction, motivation and summary of what follows in the other chapters.

Chapter Two focuses on the literature review, sources of data and definitions of Public Private Partnership, Community Development and Economic Growth. This chapter also compares PPP and Community Development concepts and looks at the lessons these might hold for Rwanda.

Chapter Three looks at why this particular research methodology was selected.

Chapter Four is the analysis, interpretation of findings and case studies. Chapter five provides conclusive remarks based on the findings.

This study concludes that in order to benefit from PPP arrangement, political backing and public and private sector buy-in are determinant factors, and that Rwanda needs to put in place proper supportive infrastructure, in the form of legislation, policies, systems, human capacity and most importantly, strong procurement controls and anti-corruption procedures. Otherwise PPP may become a vehicle for a country being exploited by shrewd Multinational corporations (MNCs) who have been in the PPP game longer than the country they are dealing with (OECD, 2008).

The last part, chapter six is references and appendices. This study follows the Harvard system of referencing.

CHAPTER TWO

2.0 LITERATURE REVIEW

Introduction

The concept of Public-Private Partnerships (PPP) is increasingly becoming important in infrastructure development and public resources management in many countries around the world. Unlike public ownership, privatisation or private ownership, PPP brings together the interests of both in a unique way (Joseph & Kelly, eds., 2000). The concept started in the United States of America and the United Kingdom of Great Britain and spread quickly to other developed economies (Savas, 2006; Link, 2006). Like the rush to privatize public enterprise in the 1980s, every country around the globe is now 'catching the PPP bug'; and from the look of things, the rush has just begun. Poor countries are looking at PPP as a means to breathe some life into their starved public infrastructure (Farlam, 2005). Even rich countries see PPP as the only way to revamp their ailing public infrastructure without raising taxes to politically sensitive levels (Savas, 2006).

The usual international agencies who pushed privatization down the throats of developing countries as a pragmatic strategy and " a tool to improve the functioning of government" (Savas, 2006: 14), the World Bank (WB) and the International Monetary Fund (IMF), are observed to be back at their game, pushing poor countries in a rush to adopt various PPP models (The World Bank Group, 2008).

The most attractive element of PPP to these countries is that it allows private money and expertise to flow into pubic sector investments and to share risks and responsibilities with private firms while ownership rights are retained or reverts to the respective government (Farlam, 2005)

But how prepared are these countries? Do they have the 'soft' infrastructure in place to support the delivery of PPP projects? What about lack of human resource capacity, negotiation weaknesses in their public sectors, procurement loopholes and endemic corruption and poor governance in some of these countries (Obama, 2009)? These are some of the serious questions officials need to ponder on before taking on this very complex concept.

It has always been argued that PPP contributes to infrastructure development, which in turn supports economic growth (IPPR, 2001; NPIP, 2009); that is the argument that has been put forward by many countries for adopting PPP. This study aims to contribute to this debate by arguing that, in fact, PPP can also be used to advance community development. While agreeing that economic growth is a necessary condition for community development, this study also attempts to clear the lingering confusion that economic growth/development (Little, 1982; Lewis, 1976) is the same as or can automatically lead to community development (Ledwith, 2005).

The study makes the point that for PPP to be successful, the government sector, the business sector, the civil society and the community, all need to come together to agree on common challenges and goals, and pursue solutions together in teamwork to achieve "triple wins" for the government, investors and local communities (Broomes, 2009).

Definition of PPP

The following definitions aim to provide the broadest understanding of this rather complex subject. To start with, Albert N. Links notes that "public-private partnership is a term of art without a precise, much less generally accepted, definition" (Link, 2006: 1). According to Emmanuel S. Savas - one of the avid proponents of privatisation and PPP - it is any arrangement between government and the private sector in which partially or traditionally public activities are performed by the private sector. Savas goes on to say that the term encompasses three different arrangements. First, it is used to denote any arrangement in which public and private sectors join together to produce and deliver goods and services. Second, it is used for complex, multi-partner, privatised, infrastructure projects. Third, it refers to a formal collaboration between business and civic leaders and local government officials to improve the urban condition (Savas, 2006). In this third case, Savas argues, corporations go beyond their usual role in the marketplace and become involved in traditionally government territory, such as schools, job training, downtown revitalisation, urban redevelopment, and much more. Government becomes more than a tax collector and provider of conventional public services and becomes a real estate developer, business lender, and so on. Religious and not-for-profit leaders add their moral authority and community outreach to the joint effort (Savas, 2006: 105-106).

In his writing, Brittan brings in 'risk sharing', a very important element in all PPPs, and defines the term as "a risk sharing relationship based upon a shared aspiration between the public sector and one or more partners to deliver a publicly agreed outcome" (Brittan, 2001:4). Other experts also say that actors in a PPP arrangement need to adopt each other's behaviours and characteristics. Governments would therefore need to think and behave like entrepreneurs, while private sector actors would need to embrace public sector interests and accept greater public accountability than they are accustomed to (Linder in Rosenau, 2000:20-21). Savas calls it the 'infusion of market principles into the political world" (Savas, 2006:318), and one could argue that the reverse is true:-politics is infused into the PPP market.

Linder explains that partnerships are viewed as a retreat from the hard-line advocacy of privatisation. From this viewpoint, Linder argues, they serve a strategic purpose, enlisting the support of more moderate elements that are less opposed to state action on principle. Linder concludes "partnerships are accommodationist; they hold back the spectre of wholesale divestiture, in exchange, promise lucrative collaboration with the state" (in Rosenau, 2000: 25).

In their definition of PPP, Linder and Rosenau add a fourth 'p' for policy and say "Public-Private Policy Partnerships speaks to a division of labour between the government and the private sector across policy spheres as much as to any specific collaboration between government and the private sector on particular policy projects" (Linder and Rosenau, 2000:1)

International and Multilateral organisations have also made attempts to define PPP from their own perspectives. The OECD (Organisation for Economic Cooperation & Development) defines a public-private partnership as an agreement between the government and one or more private partners (which may include the operators and the financers) according to which the private partners deliver the service in such a manner that the service delivery objectives of the government are aligned with the profit objectives of the private partners and where the effectiveness of the alignment depends on a sufficient transfer of risk to the private partners (OECD, 2008).

According to the International Monetary Fund (IMF, 2004:4), public-private partnerships (PPPs) refer to arrangements where the private sector supplies infrastructure assets and services that traditionally have been provided by the government. In addition to private execution and financing of public investment, PPPs have two other important characteristics: there is an emphasis on service provision, as well as investment, by the private sector; and significant risk is transferred from the government to the private sector.

For the European Investment Bank (EIB, 2004:2), "public-private partnership" is a
generic term for the relationships formed between the private sector and public bodies often with the aim of introducing private sector resources and/or expertise in order to help provide and deliver public sector assets and services. The term PPP is thus used to describe a wide variety of working arrangements from loose, informal and strategic partnerships, to design-build-

finance-and-operate (DBFO) type service contracts and formal joint venture companies.

The Canadian Council for Public Private Partnerships (CCPPP) defines PPP as a cooperative venture between the public and private sectors, built on the expertise of each partner, which best meets clearly defined public needs through the appropriate allocation of resources, risks and rewards (CCPPP online, n.d)

Each industry also defines PPP from its own viewpoint and a few industry definitions will suffice here. The credit rating company Standard and Poor's (S&P) definition of a PPP is any medium- to long-term relationship between the public and private sectors, involving the sharing of risks and rewards of multi-sector skills, expertise and finance to deliver desired policy outcomes (S &P, 2005, quoted in OECD, 2008).

The U.S Department of Transportation (DOT) defines PPP as contractual agreements formed between a public agency and private sector entity that allow for greater private participation in the delivery of transport projects. DOT goes on to explain that, unlike conventional methods of contracting for a project, in which discrete functions are divided and procured through separate solicitations, PPPs contemplate a single private entity being responsible and financially liable for performing all or a significant number of functions in connection with a project. It adds that the private sector partner is typically a consortium of private companies with expertise in the different functions to be performed, such as design, construction, financing, operation and/or maintenance; the public sector agency shifts certain risks to the private partner and focuses on desired outcomes instead of detailed project specifications, and the private partner receives the opportunity to earn a financial return commensurate with the risks it assumes. Some of the risks assumed by the private sector partner may include financial risks like equity investment, liability for indebtedness, a fixed priced contract, or a combination; risks related to design, construction, operation and maintenance (DOT/FHWA, 2003).

Finally, Rwanda's own definition is a "contractual arrangements between the public and private sector under which the private firm delivers a public infrastructure asset and/or a public service in return for payments from government and /or users, government guarantees and /or any other form of government contribution with a fiscal impact" (NPIP, 2009:13).

In summary, therefore, public-private partnership means joint initiatives for public sector in conjunction with the private, for-profit and not-for-profit sectors, also known as the government, business and civil society sectors (Savas, 2006). We also learn that within these partnerships, each of the actors adopts each other's behaviours and characteristics, contributes resources such as finance, human, technical, and intangibles such as political support, information, moral authority and community outreach. Other characteristics of PPP arrangements included risk sharing and shared decision-making. Further more we learn that the purpose of partnerships is to mobilise national resources and efforts toward achieving national objectives, such as economic development and social progress.

But are the above reasons enough to explain why these sectors, whose territories and roles are traditionally defined and marked, are finally clamouring to join their efforts and resources? In other words, have these reasons just emerged?

A look at the history and origins of PPP will shed some more light at the forces behind this new paradigm in public resources management (Corry, in Ghobadian *et al*, eds., 2004).

A Brief History of PPP

It is difficult to pinpoint exactly when PPP started, because governments have always cooperated with the private sector, in one way or the other, and one can rightly argue that this relationship naturally evolved into modern day PPP. But many experts agree that the concept of Public-Private Partnership can be traced in the United States of America (USA) as far as 16th and 17th centuries (Link, 2006).

Link (2006) argues that most partnerships between government and the private sector are formed to achieve national objectives, which may vary from scientific research and development to national security.

Experts agree that PPP helps to bring fragmented resources together (Savas, 2000) to achieve national goals, and Link (2006) gives examples of how the two World Wars forced western governments to form partnerships with the private sector institutions to mobilise resources for the war effort. At the end of World War II, US President Roosevelt sought to exploit partnerships built and knowledge gained for economic benefits, writing to the director of The Office of Scientific Research and Development (OSR&D):

"there is... no reason why the lessons to be found in this experiment cannot be profitably employed in times of peace.....for the improvement of the national health, the creation of new enterprises bringing new jobs, and the betterment of the national standard of living" (quoted in Link, 2006:17). Further evidence shows that successive U.S governments continued to put partnerships with the private sector in R&D at the centre of their economic agenda. For example President Clinton stated after his election in 1993, that "government can play a key role in helping private firms develop and profit from innovations" (quoted in Rosenau, 2000:38).

In continental Europe, according to the European Investment Bank (EIB) the term Public Private Partnership has been in general use since the 1990s; but there is no single European model of a PPP (EIB, 2004). However, before PPP, EIB argues, there was a strong tradition in Europe of risk sharing concession structures between the public and private sectors.

Ghobadian *et al*, (2004) argues that the practice of conceding some public services to private sector providers goes centuries back. In France for example the system of using 'financial investors' to deliver public works was common during the 16th and 17th centuries, which included riverbed and canal construction, paving roads, waste collection, public lighting, mail distribution and public transportation (Ghobadian et al, eds., 2004). After the Second

World War several countries including Britain, Italy, France, Japan and the US started to use public franchise holders to construct toll motorway networks, which continued through out 1960s and 1970s, according to Ghobadian, *et al*. In these cases, however, the private entity was only contracted to carry out public works, with no responsibility for financing, designing, management or sharing the risk with the public sector. But OECD argues that the introduction of PPP in the early 1990s established a mode of public service delivery that redefined the roles of the public and private sectors (OECD, 2008).

The modern form of PPP began to take shape in Britain for ideological reasons, after the Conservative Party under Margaret Thatcher took power in 1979, according to Redwood (2004). The Conservatives sought to end the nationalisation of key industries and state involvement in the production and delivery of goods and services. The Local Government Planning and Land Act 1980 and the Local Government Act 1988 required the local authorities to submit a range of public services to compulsory tendering and award the delivery to the lowest bidder.

"The market testing concept" was extended to the National Health Service (NHS) in 1983, and the Private Finance Initiative (PFI), a form of PPP preferred in Britain, was fully introduced in 1992. The key features of the new PFI were:

- ❖ to allow any privately financed project that could operate profitably to proceed without comparing them with a similar project in the public sector;

- ❖ to actively encourage joint ventures with the private sector, where these involve a sensible transfer of risk to the private sector; and
- ❖ to allow greater use of leasing where it offered value for money (Ghobadian, et al, eds., 2004).

The Labour administration that assumed power under Tony Blair as prime minister in 1997, continued with the PPP approach, which they had developed in 1994 while in opposition. According to the Rt. Hon John Redwood MP:

"the government wants to spend huge sums of money on new offices, new public bodies, new railway lines, schools, hospitals, prisons, houses and many other facilities. It sees the PFI as the answer to their prayers. They thought they could keep the big capital costs off the government balance sheet" *(Redwood, in Ghobadian et al, 2004:19).*

"The core objective for the public sector of a PPP programme is to harness private sector skills in support of improved public sector services" (Andrew Smith, Chief Secretary, HM Treasury, 2000:5)

O'Brien, (1997:32)) asserts that Partnerships became a "cross-party" concept in Britain (quoted by Falconer and McLaughlin in Osborne, 2000:122).

In developing countries, in late 1980s and early 1990s the IMF and World Bank started shifting from promoting privatisation of state-owned enterprises to private sector involvement in infrastructure (The World Bank Group, 2008).

Today governments every where are partnering with the private sector to deliver a wider spectrum of goods and services to the public and PPP has become embedded in public service management. There are even suggestions to make PPP sharia law-compliant for Muslim countries (Davie, 2008).

Advantages, spectrum and models of PPP

In order to understand the benefits of PPP, one needs to look at the alternatives that have been tried in the past: Public ownership and full privatization, leading to private ownership of former public enterprises. Each alternative has its own strengths as well weaknesses, but PPP proponents say it brings together the best of both worlds.

PPP have been credited with bringing in the public sector a businesslike approach to budgeting and decision-making, and infusing business characteristics into the world of public policy (Pike, in Joseph & Kelly, eds., 2000).

The United Nations Development Programme (UNDP, 2004) states that PPP offer an alternative to full privatization by combining the advantages of both the public and private sectors, such as:

- social responsibility, environmental awareness and public accountability of the public sector; and
- finance, technology, managerial efficiency and entrepreneurial spirit of the private sector.

According to Falconer and McLaughlin (in Osborne, 2000:121) the use of public private partnership arrangements has a number of important advantages: the need to provide alternative sources of capital funding for the public sector; the need to 'reinvent' government and establish legitimacy with local communities in the implementation of local economic development policies; and the need to address the challenge posed by the increasing involvement and participation in the policy process of the civil society organisations.

In an open letter to President-elect Barack Obama, the US National Council for Public-Private Partnerships (NCPPP) stated that:

"PPPs are recognized as an innovative method of funding infrastructure projects to best reduce costs, accelerate delivery, create jobs, and transfer risks to the private sector-all while providing high quality projects". And urged the new President to recognize PPPs "as an important option in addressing the nation's infrastructure needs, and provide a much needed economic stimulus" (NCPPP, 2008).

One of the strongest arguments in favour of PPP is aptly put by Rosenau that "government does some things best, the private sector other things, and the not-for-profit still does best different things. PPP combines the best of each" (Rosenau, 2000:218).

The old justification for government's monopoly of public services, argues Savas, was that these were so vital, benefit so many people, and requires so much capital that the private sector could not be entrusted with this responsibility and it lacks resources of this magnitude. In modern economic setting, however, this argument cannot stand any scrutiny. Savas calls this "curious reasoning". "Facilities so vital to a nation's economy should be encouraged with incentives to attract investment in viable projects, priced according to supply and demand rather than politics, operated efficiently, and maintained in good condition" (Savas, 2006:237).

Savas (2006) also argues that the need for infrastructure has outstripped the supply of conventional public funds, and private groups are increasingly sought to finance, design, build, operate and even own infrastructure via innovative public private partnerships. This is happening right across a wide spectrum of public service sectors such as transportation, water-supply systems and waste-water treatment plants, telecommunications & ICT, electricity generation and distribution, defence and security, fire and disaster management, education, judiciary and criminal justice, healthcare, public housing, regeneration and community development and many more. Simply put, there are few public service sectors that are out of bounds to PPP in today's world. The IMF names "non-contractible" services such as national defence, maintenance of public law and order, and diplomatic service, although these also have contractible elements of their services (IMF, 2004:11).

According to the Canadian Council for PPP (CCPPP online, n.d), Public-private partnerships span a spectrum of models that progressively engage the expertise or capital of the private sector. At one end, there is straight contracting out as an alternative to traditionally delivered public services. At the other end, there are arrangements that are publicly administered but within a framework that allows for private finance, design, building, operation and possibly temporary ownership of an asset. This brings in the public sector innovation, efficiency and effectiveness usually associated with the private sector.

According to Claude V. Chang (2006), the inefficiency of the public sector stems from information asymmetries; organisation paralysis and policy drift; and poor management. Information asymmetry, Chang argues, arises from different objectives between the principal (government) and agent (the manager); and inadequate monitoring system; while organisation paralysis and policy drift result when recommended action is potentially unfavourable to politicians or is not in accordance with the bureaucrat's agenda. PPP allows the private sector's efficient management style, money and expertise to flow into pubic sector investments while ownership rights are retained or reverts to the public sector (Farlam, 2005). PPP may therefore be used by governments to plug gaps in the public finances (IMF, 2004); hence avoiding the politically risky tax raises (Collin & Hanson, in Osborne, 2000). This is known as off-balance sheet borrowing (Gosling, 2004).

According to US Federal Highway Administration, as PPPs have become more common, many governments have become eager to capitalise on the increased efficiencies of the private sector and have found that private developers deliver greater value for money, (FHWA, 2009). Proponents of this argument say resource wastage is endemic in the public sector and PPP could provide quality services at less cost than traditional public sector procurement (Savas, 2006).

OECD states that sufficient transfer of risk to the private partner is necessary to ensure efficiency and value for money; and that "for the transfer of risk to be most effective, risk must also be transferred to the party best able to carry it" (OECD, 2008: 13).

In the health sector for example, many countries started looking for private sector partners to secure value for money and share some of the risks associated with service delivery, after realising that health services are taking a large and growing share of the national resources (Abel-Smith, 1976). Abel-Smith argues that as an increasing proportion of health service bill continue to fall on governments, more and more countries are searching for ways to contain the cost and secure better value for money. Countries, both rich and poor are faced with questions such as "how much are costs increasing and why are they increasing? How is it possible to contain cost and secure better value for all the money which is spent" (Abel-Smith, 1976:121).

The British government's handbook on creating PPPs through market testing and contracting out defines value for money as "better quality services for customers at optimal cost to taxpayers" (HMSO, 1998:9). According to Anthony Smith (2007) value for money means the optimum combination of whole life costs and quality. This does not mean the cheapest. Smith argues that VfM is best achieved by:

- ❖ Reducing the cost and time of procurement
- ❖ Improving project, contract and asset management
- ❖ Competition-using competitive procurement
- ❖ Making use of the size of government purchasing power
- ❖ Use of continuous improvement
- ❖ Using the best procurement process

In most countries, value for money in PPP projects is measured against the " public Sector Comparator" (PSC), which is a hypothetical estimate of how much the project would have cost through conventional public sector procurement methods (Gosling, 2004; 0ECD, 2008). In Britain for example, PFI projects were found to be saving between 3-12% of project costs against the PSC (IPPR, 2001). An Arthur Andersen study for the Treasury suggested that the VfM gains could be as much as 10-20% (cited in Brittan, 2001). 76% of PFI projects were completed on time against 30% in conventional procurement, and 78% of PFI projects were completed on budget against 27% in conventional procurement (NAO, 2003b, quoted in Gosling, 2004:35). However, the IPPR Commission on PPP (2001) also found that road and prison PFIs were likely to offer more significant savings than hospital PFI projects. PPP in IT has been found to be a total failure and abandoned by the British government (Gosling, 2004).

Concerns have also been raised on the assessment of VfM against a non-existent (hypothetical) PSC, and that PSC is subjective and likely to be manipulated in favour of PFI projects (Gosling, 2004:29-33). The potential for subjectivity and manipulation springs from the fact that once PPP receives full political backing, there is likely to be a bias to prove that it works better than traditional procurement methods (IPPR, 2001). Gosling also argues that there are paper advantages to departments in achieving off-balance sheet treatment that bias the procurement process towards PFI. Quoting Timmins (2002), Gosling asserts "the perception that comparators were 'rigged' or 'fiddled' in order to allow the smooth process of PFI projects in the face of the lack of an alternative took a firmer hold in public debate" (2004:29; 43).

For PPP to succeed in Rwanda and other developing countries, they will have to avoid "poor-designed approaches" that characterised privatisation in those countries (Chang, 2006: 13).

It is these poor approaches to privatization that have led many in developing parts of the world to believe that the benefits went to Multinational Corporations (MNC) from developed countries. "Now the less developed world sees that some benefits of privatisation in poor nations have often gone to well-off countries" President Paul Kagame of Rwanda told a Commonwealth Business Council conference in London, (Kimenyi, 2009). This view is supported by Chang who argues that one of the reasons behind the West's push for privatisation in developing countries was the "creation of investment opportunities for Western investors while raising cash to service external debts" (Chang, 2006:79).

Public private partnerships are delivered through one of the following models:

Design-Build (DB): A private sector entity is contracted to design and build infrastructure to meet public sector performance specifications, often for a fixed price, so the risk of cost overruns is transferred to the private sector.

Operation & Maintenance Contract (O & M): A private sector operator is contracted to operate and maintain a publicly-owned asset for a specified period of time. Ownership of the asset remains with the public entity.

Design-Build-Finance-Operate (DBFO): A private sector entity, under contract, designs, finances and constructs a new facility under a long-term contract, and operates the facility during that term. The private partner transfers the new facility to the public sector at the end of the contracted term.

Build-Own-Operate (BOO): A private sector entity finances, builds, owns and operates a facility or service permanently. The public interests are stated in the original agreement and through on-going regulatory authority.

Build-Own-Operate-Transfer (BOOT): A private sector entity is given a franchise to finance, design, build and operate a facility (and to charge user fees) for a specified period, after which ownership is transferred back to the public sector.

Buy-Build-Operate (BBO): Transfer of a public asset to a private or quasi-public entity usually under contract that the assets are to be upgraded and operated for a specified period of time. Public control is exercised through the contract at the time of transfer.

Operation License: A private operator is given a license or rights to operate a public service, usually for a specified term. This is commonly used in IT projects.

Lease/Develop/Operate (LDO) or Build/Develop/Operate (BDO): Under these partnerships arrangements, the private sector entity leases or buys an existing facility from a public sector agency; invests its own capital to renovate, modernise, and/or expand the facility; and then operates it under a contract with the public agency.

Finance Only: A private entity, usually a financial services company, funds a project directly or uses various mechanisms such as a long-term lease or bond issue (Classification by CCPPP online, n.d).

These models represent just examples rather than a complete listing as PPP are designed differently in different countries and under different circumstances.

Within the above spectrum, PPPs can be categorised based on the extent of public and private sector involvement and the degree of risk allocation, as indicated in *figure 1*.

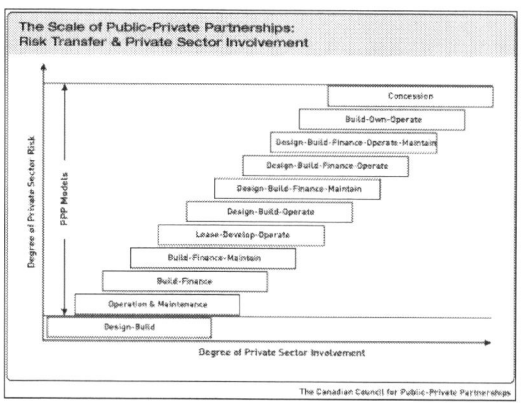

Figure 1: Models of PPP. *Source:* CCPPP www.pppcouncil.ca

Weaknesses and Limitations of PPP

However, despite all associated advantages, PPP policies everywhere have not passed without strong critics and opposition. Charges against PPP are many, especially coming from Trade Unions and other campaigning groups. In Britain, public sector union UNISON has been consistent in pressurising the government to abandon PFI, calling it a waste of taxpayers' money. In one report entitled *A Policy Built on Sand* (Pollock, *et al*, 2005) the union disproves the claim that the extra costs of PFI are offset by increased efficiency and thereby undermines the government's arguments for its continued use to build hospitals, schools and other major public sector projects.

UNISON Secretary General Dave Prentis said that the report knocks out another of the government's chief arguments for its continued use, namely that it generates value for money by improving the efficiency of construction procurement, calling the government's evidence used to justify this claim selective and fatally flawed (*CNPLUS, 2005*). Campaigners against PPP also charge that cost shifting is a serious problem affecting PPP projects. They argue that with a mixed public-private system, there is a great danger that the private sector providers will gravitate towards the services where it is easy to make a quick profit, leaving the public sector carrying the inherently unprofitable activities, and once again being dubbed "inefficient" (Barker, 1996: 155, cited in Rosenau, 2000:231).

Critics also allege that the savings associated with PPP are achieved through pay cuts and poor conditions for workers (Corry, D., in Ghobadian *et al*, eds. 2004).

Lack of accountability is another charge levelled against PPP. The argument is that PPP negatively affects the ways in which public services are held to account (IPPR, 2001). "Political responsibility is clearly disrupted by long-term PPP contracts with the private sector" (Gosling, 2004:82). Gosling argues that, for example, if voters wanted to change the type of school meals provided under a 25-year PFI schools contract no longer have recourse to the local ballot box to bring about the change they desire.

The IPPR report concluded that accountability issues such as transparency, responsibility and responsiveness need to be given serious consideration in PPP projects (IPPR, 2001).

Political theorists argue that partnerships should be avoided because of regressive political dynamics they create. Their argument is that, less direct public provision of services will lead to a more privatised society, the erosion of non-market values, and, eventually, a reduced willingness on the part of citizens to fund public services (IPPR, 2001: 29).

A case has also been made against private sector involvement in education sector as "gradual encroachment of privatization" (Lissauer and Robinson, eds. 2000:1).

According to Redwood, the PPP path leads to the transfer of ownership and control of public infrastructure and leaves to the private sector "virtually all decision-making authority over what investment will be made and when" (in Ghobadian, *et al.* eds., 2004:21).

Many more criticisms are levelled against PPP than can be covered by this study, but they include poor quality of services, conflict of interest, equity and access issues- that vulnerable groups may lose out, PPPs may actually lead to increased cost of projects, lack of democracy and participation and increased rather than reduced regulation (Rosenau, 2000).

Keys to success or failure of PPP

NCPPP (2008) outlines six critical components of any successful Public Private partnership as, political leadership or 'commitment from the top', public sector involvement, a well thought out plan, a dedicated income stream, communications with stakeholders, and selecting the right partner.

According to Geoffrey Hamilton (UNECE, 2008) a coherent PPP policy, strong enabling institutions, a good legal framework, cooperative risk sharing and mutual support, transparency, putting people first and achieving sustainable development are the important elements to guarantee the success of partnerships.

Hamilton advises that protracted negotiations and lack of the above elements may lead to cancellation of projects and failure of PPP. A World Bank report in 2008 highlighted two projects that were cancelled in Mozambique and Rwanda in 2007, due to contractual misunderstandings or violations; and in total 31 projects were cancelled or 'distressed' in Sub-Saharan Africa between 1990 and 2007 (The World Bank, 2008:3).

Conflict of interest is another element that could ruin PPP, and may arise when public officials have interest in a PPP project they are handling. One such case that is likely not to be isolated in Africa, is Uganda's Entebbe airport PPP with Dodsal Group of Dubai, in which the Group is supposed to be granted a 10-year concession to upgrade and run the country's only international airport. Media reports in Uganda alleged that various officials in ministries of Works, Foreign Affairs and Finance had business interests associated with the airport operations and this was creating confusion and affecting the airport PPP (Obore, 2009; Kasasira, 2009).

This case in Uganda also highlights the importance of prior stakeholder consultation. A government minister was quoted as saying that the project was supposed to be a BOT (build, operate transfer) type procurement, but problems arose because some stakeholders were only informed when the project was already in progress (Kasasira, 2009).

To John Davie, Chairman of United Kingdom Trade & Investment's (UKTI) PPP Export Advisory Group and Head of International Business Development at Vector Management International Limited, PPP needs high level political support- and it must be communicated to lower levels of government- to succeed. He argues for the building of an informed debate, development of private sector capacity and the use of recognized international procedures and contracts in order to attract international finance and highest quality management (Davie, 2008).

According to the UNDP (2004) guidelines on successful partnerships, government, businesses and community leaders must understand and respect one another's goals. For instance: the government may initially have difficulty accepting the profit motive of private businesses; the private companies may be tempted to walk away from the more bureaucratic decision-making processes used in the public sector; and/or local communities may not have the patience needed to address issues affecting other areas of the city.

Other problems that may derail or ruin PPP include the reciprocal mistrust between the public and private sectors, lack of understanding of each other's interests, the absence of locally available information on, and experience with, arranging sustainable partnerships; and the underlying legal, political and institutional obstacles to forming effective public private partnerships (Huxman and Vangen, in Osborne, 2000). Managing trust and power relations between partners may determine the success or failure of PPP. "Perceptions about the power differences play a very significant role in hampering trust building" (Huxman and Vangen, in Osborne, 2000: 298).

UNDP (2004) argues that these obstacles often lead to lengthy negotiations, increased transaction costs, and make smaller projects much less attractive to potential investors. In order to minimise the harm from such obstacles, PPP arrangements should provide certain safeguards for the public and private sectors and for the community.

Community Development

The National Occupational Standards (NOS) for community development work in England defines community development (CD) by its purpose:

The key purpose of CD is collectively to bring about social change and justice by working with communities to:

- Identify their needs, opportunities, rights and responsibilities
- Plan, organise and take action
- Evaluate the effectiveness and impact of the action
- …all in ways which challenge oppression and tackle inequalities.

NOS also define CD work by its values, which are:

- *Social justice*: working towards a fairer society that respects civil and human rights, and challenges oppression
- *Self-determination*: individuals and groups have the right to identify

shared issues and concerns as the starting point for collective action

- *Working and learning together:* valuing and using the skills, knowledge, experience and diversity within communities to collectively bring about desired changes
- *Sustainable communities*: empowering communities to develop their independence and autonomy, whilst making and maintaining links to the wider society
- *Participation:* everyone has the right to fully participate in the decision-making processes that affect their lives
- *Reflective practice*: effective CD is informed and enhanced through reflection on action (NOS, 2001).

Community development is also defined as a set of values and practices which play a special role in overcoming poverty and disadvantage, knitting society together at the grass roots and deepening democracy (Department for Communities and Local Government, 2007:13).

The Community Development Challenge (CDC) also defines CD by what it does that other Occupations don't do. It argues that what distinguishes community development from other occupations is that it pursues objectives in all six components illustrated in the NOS values, above, starting with the identification of key local issues and working through to assisting partnership between communities and public bodies. It acknowledges that taken individually, these principles do not belong to community development alone; but it is the only profession that interweaves and concentrates these together and applies certain techniques to realize them. It's only CD that:

- Creates and facilitates opportunities for communities and local authorities to discuss strategies for addressing their needs
- Identifies and supports community members to take on more active and responsible roles
- Helps organisations to establish informal networks and ensures that they take on appropriate structures
- Provides advice on constitutions, legal requirements and resourcing
- Sets up and services strategic forums that bring together people and groups with a common agenda or similar life experiences
- Encourages groups to think about people in their communities who find it difficult to participate in their organisation, and helps organisations to change or to develop new activities and services that are more inclusive and accessible (CDC, 2007:16).

If an organisation or individual is involved in all the above, together, not separately, that's called community development.

It follows therefore that CD work should be about what the community wants and how they want it, as opposed to what authorities or funders want.

According to Taylor et al (2000) CD takes place predominantly in those communities that face disadvantage and discrimination. "It is particularly concerned to challenge the individual prejudices and institutional discrimination that isolate, divide and exclude people from their communities and society at large" (Taylor et al, 2000:9).

ABCD (Achieving Better Community Development) identifies CD as an activity that confronts disadvantage, poverty and exclusion, and promotes values of active citizenship, learning, and community participation (Barr & Hashagen, 2000).

Community Development vs. Economic Growth

Economic Growth, on the other hand, is about the growth of output per head of population, not about distribution (Lewis, 1976). "It is possible that output may be growing, and yet that the mass of the people may be becoming poorer" (Lewis, 1976:9). Lewis argues that economic growth does not mean increased consumption; output may be growing while consumption is declining, either because saving is increasing, or because the government is using up more output for its own purposes. He states the three proximate causes of economic growth as: economic activity, increasing knowledge, and increasing capital (Lewis, 1976:23).

According to an award-winning article on UN's Millennium Development Goals (MDGs) by Ugandan journalist Richard M. Kavuma despite Uganda's impressive economic growth rates, averaging 6% throughout the 1990s, majority Ugandans remained among the poorest. Kavuma argues that while Kampala, the capital city is teeming with new office blocks, residential bungalows and the latest car models, the poorest were going with out food (Kavuma, 2006).

Community development advocates would strongly despise this type of development or growth. Instead CD advocates for the building up of social capital, which is "transferable and transformative" (Ledwith, 2005:2). According to Ledwith, where there is CD the hopelessness that normally gives rise to anger, violence or apathy becomes a more dignified and determined hopefulness, where communities are defined by confidence, critical consciousness and collectivity.

Community development should not be taken to be anti-economic growth; in fact this study argues that economic growth is a necessary condition for community development to take place. But since emphasis on per capita economic growth has not delivered real development in developing countries (Kimanuka, 2008), this study asserts that a shift to CD principles will deliver sustainable and inclusive growth (Broomes, 2009). CD, according to Taylor *et al* (2000) promotes growth with change, where people have more power over the changes that are taking place around them, the policies that affect them, and the services they use. In other words, CD principles help to ensure that people are in charge of that growth, and its benefits are distributed fairly.

In his definition of economic development Ian M.D Little (1982) seeks to integrate it with welfare economics:

"Economic development (or economic progress or real economic growth) occurs if there is a rise in the present value of average (weighted) consumption per head. The future starts now, and consumption is measured at market prices or at the maximum prices people would be willing to pay for what they consume" (Little, 1982:6). Even this definition would not satisfy CD practice, as it indicates that people are still at the mercy of market forces rather than being in charge of their own destiny.

Ledwith (2005) argues that grassroots liberation, participatory democracy and social justice, rather than domination by the market or the state, should be at the heart of CD practice.

Ira Shor (in Ledwith, 2005) makes a point that since the end of the Cold War multinational conglomerates have wielded enormous power, which they have used to unilaterally rewrite the social contract. As a result, he argues:

"a religion of the marketplace has emerged whereby market forces are considered too sacred to be touched by local and social concerns; human needs that contradict market needs are fast becoming expendable; indeed it appears that the market religion is superseding regional planning, community desires and elected governments at all levels" (in Ledwith, 2005: viii). Shor continues to argue that to counter this power that has collected in the hands of a few world businesses, communities, citizens, and families need to educate and organise themselves in order to protect their political rights, their livelihoods, homes, neighbourhoods, children, health and environment, and this can be achieved through community development (in Ledwith, 2005) .

Lack of CD, according to *The Community Development Challenge,* is manifested in the following situation:

- ❖ There is often lack of or few community groups, many individuals do not realise that the issues that concern them are shared by others and can be resolved by joint actions;

❖ The most disadvantaged people receive poor quality public services yet are least confident and skilled at representing their needs to authorities;

❖ Some of the groups that do exist remain small and exclusive, dominated by cliques or strong individuals who keep decision-making (and sometimes benefits) to themselves; organisations may be run unconstitutionally or unfairly;

❖ Community organisations fail to adapt to changing circumstances or miss out on funding opportunities which might enable them to expand or change direction. Their work becomes unsustainable or inappropriate and doesn't evolve;

❖ Community leaders and representatives are not properly selected and held accountable and may flounder or be ineffective on partnership boards;

❖ Different interests in communities are unable to reach a consensus or vision that articulates their views to others and as a consequence their interests do not register in public decision-making;

❖ Sections of the local population are not able to participate in activities that are intended for the whole community because prejudices, assumptions and cultural differences are not tackled;

❖ Public agencies and departments that need to engage with local communities are unaware of each other's efforts, lack insight into how communities work and have few channels for dialogue with them (Department for Communities and Local Government, *DCLG, 2007:10*).

This study argues that the above situation is mostly a result of top-down planning that does not incorporate community development principles. Figure 2, below attempts to elaborate the sequence of events that may result in the above scenario.

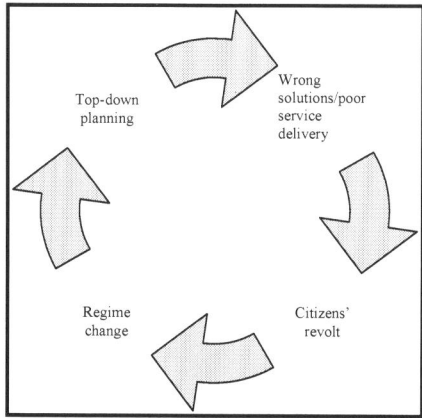

Figure 2: The Vicious Cycle of Top-down Planning Model. Source: Author

CD practice requires government's shift from a deliverer of goods and services to an enabler- enabling and empowering communities to take charge of their own lives. Inevitably this shift can create resistance and invites tensions. But community development also helps people and public institutions to respond positively to this transformation by creating additional avenues of participation and "releasing new energies from below" (, *DCLG, 2007:8*).

NOS advocates for the development of strategic relationships with communities and organizations, and within partnerships- this is important because CD "values inclusive collaborative working in bringing about strategic change" (NOS, 2001:10)

PPP vs. Community Development

It can be argued that PPP presents a unique opportunity for public authorities and businesses to engage and involve local communities in what they do, and together to address some of the concerns of community development (IPPR, 2001).

This study argues that in addition to using PPP in pursuit of economic growth, Rwanda's PPP could be modelled in a way that puts high consideration to community development and incorporates some of CD's core principles and values, and PPP projects designed in a way that ensures they are responsive to communities and reflect the needs of local people. PPP projects, according to Rosenau, may perform well if there is "broad community or societal consensus in the value of the policy goals" (Rosenau, 2000: 232). Indeed there are plenty of examples where PPP projects were designed without the involvement of local communities and ended up in failure (IPPR, 2001).

Stiglitz and Wallsten (1999:61-62) observed that:

"Programs that attempt to select projects only on their economic and scientific merits may never develop a constituency and, thus, political support" (cited in Rose*nau*, 2000:232). The thrust of Stiglitz and Wallsten's argument is that PPP projects should not only aim at correcting market failures or to advance science and economic growth, but also to address the local needs of the community where they operate.

The IPPR report (2001) argues that PPPs open up new possibilities for community engagement because:

- ❖ It reconfigures services and focuses on outcomes; PPPs create an opportunity for service planners and purchasers to reconsider traditional modes of governance and delivery
- ❖ Partnerships create new challenges for public accountability by devolving authority over decision-making and public expenditure to non-elected partnerships. This creates the need for new and robust forms of accountability and community engagement can help address the potential legitimacy deficit of some PPPs
- ❖ PPPs offer an ambitious vision for local people themselves to be partners.

The IPPR recommends, therefore, that it is important to allow those affected to be involved in shaping the nature of the partnership arrangement, and ensure that outcomes and outputs "genuinely reflect the needs and expectations of citizens and service users" (IPPR, 2001:213).

However, for local people to be effective in engaging with PPP, they need to be empowered. It is therefore important that initiatives aimed at empowering local communities are part of PPP implementation process.

Community empowerment is a central element in community

development practice, because it gives the community the knowledge, the skills and the ability to initiate change as well as take ownership and manage that change.

Lessons for Rwanda

The above arguments are Western justifications for PPP and CD. What lessons for a poor country like Rwanda, with a history of violence and exclusion, and where community development is lacking?

Community development in Rwanda is firmly anchored on the "Community Development Policy" adopted by the Rwandan Cabinet in March 2001 and revised in April 2008, with the "overarching goal of ensuring effective and sustainable participation of the community in its own development, in order to achieve poverty reduction and self-reliance based on the sustainable exploitation of available resources" (Republic of Rwanda, Ministry of Local Government, Community Development Policy, revised version April, 2008).

The policy was formulated in response to the challenges the community is still confronted with, which are listed as: extreme poverty, illiteracy, a culture of deference to authority, and the widespread use of traditional farming methods which constrain significant sustainable development. The document adds "Community Development is essentially about building the capacity of the community to solve its own problems" (Minaloc, 2008:4). This is a very important statement as far as community development is concerned. In other words, the community development policy as a whole captures most of the important pillars of community development practice, although the government doing it in a top-down planning fashion.

The government - rather than the community itself - still very much drives community development in Rwanda. The policy document discussed above was passed by the cabinet and is being implemented by the Ministry of Local Government, which is an agent of central government. The problems the community faces as indicated in the document, were analysed and agreed upon by the government, apparently at the central level. One could say exactly the same about the Community Development Challenge, produced by DLCG in the UK.

There is no reference in the document to prior consultation with the community affected, which is a very important pillar of community development practice.

However, the ministry of local government states that the community development policy was drawn up with the participation of different actors in Rwanda including civil society, the private sector, institutions of higher learning, and individuals involved in development work in Rwanda (Community Development Policy, 2008)

Rwanda also has a policy of requiring all NGOs and donor agencies in the country to align their policy aims and objectives in support of development policies set by the government. To this effect the United Nations Development Programme (UNDP) is one of the agencies supporting the government's community development agenda and is partnering with the government in

Rwanda Millennium Development Villages project, which is defined as 'a new bottom-up approach to lift developing country villages out of poverty trap that afflicts more than one billion people worldwide" (UNDP, 2009). The UN agency in March 2009 advertised the recruitment of five "Community Development Facilitators" who will facilitate the community's engagement and leadership in project planning and activities (UNDP 26 March 2009).

All CD experts and activists agree that CD begins with the process of empowerment through conscious-raising and grows through participation in local issues (Ledwith, 2005; Gilchrist, 2006; Taylor, Barr &West, 2000). Empowerment involves critical education that encourages people to question their reality (Ledwith, 2005). Community development policies everywhere have probably been, at some point and in one way or another, initiated or driven by governments or their agents, before the community is empowered to take responsibility. The Department for Communities and Local Government (DCLG) does pretty much the same in the UK (*DCLG, 2007*), although communities here are mature and avenues for their participation and involvement are much developed and widespread than one would expect to find in Rwanda.

The community development policy in Rwanda refers to some of the obstacles it has to overcome before communities can be empowered to fully participate in and take responsibility for their own development. These include extreme poverty, illiteracy, a culture of deference to authority, and the widespread use of traditional farming methods. The "culture of deference to authority" means that people have been used to being told what to do by the authority, in a top-down approach. The role of community development is also to challenge established power structures. But there must be steps and stages taken to match from that culture to a culture of participation, involvement and responsibility. The community development policy, obviously engineered and championed by the government, appears to be the beginning of what could be a long road to achieving community development objectives in Rwanda. Indeed one of the principal objectives of Rwanda's community development policy is to 'foster public participation in a bid to turn around the centralistic development approach that had previously characterised the country" (Community Development Policy, 2008:4).

The Government of Rwanda (GoR) has also embarked on a decentralisation process since 2003 (MINALOC, 2003), which is part of empowering local communities to take responsibility and make decisions for their own development.

Taylor et al argue that 'giving up power' "through sharing it with communities can actually and paradoxically be empowering for all those concerned- a positive, rather than a zero sum game, where both parties benefit" (Taylor, et al, 2000:10)

Rwanda's Ministry of Local Government, in whose docket community development and social welfare also falls, is responsible for implementing the policy, and has set up community development administrative structures from the Cell up to the District level.[2] The government has also established a community development fund (CDF) to support community development initiatives.

This study argues that the above efforts to entrench community development in Rwanda could be boosted by incorporating the ABCD (Achieving Better Community Development) framework in order to properly evaluate the effectiveness of CD policies and strategies.

The ABCD approach has three key ideas:

1. The cycle of change
2. The pyramid of outcomes
3. The steps to implementation

The cycle of change focuses on:

- ❖ Personal empowerment: individual learning, knowledge, confidence and skill.
- ❖ Positive action: specific work to identify and involve groups excluded by poverty, health, race, gender or disability and to challenge established power structures.
- ❖ Community organisation: includes general activity in the community, the range, quality and effectiveness of community-based groups

---

[2] *Local administration in Rwanda is organised from Umudugudu (village), Akagari (Cell), Umurenge (Sector) up to Akarere (District) level (Community Development Policy, 2008:5).*

and organisations, and the nature and quality of their relationships with each other and the wider world.

- ❖ Participation and influence: through which change in the circumstances of community life is achieved (Barr and Hashagen, 2000)

The ABCD approach argues that evaluation is a central part to effective performance, and in community development activities, it should be conducted with communities themselves. In this way, a shared view about what change needs to take place and how that will occur can be developed.

The ABCD model, which is a general framework for planning, evaluating and learning from community development interventions, puts sustainable communities and good quality of life for members of the community at the centre of community development.

Figure 3, below sets out the key relationships in the ABCD model. Along the bottom are the four dimensions of community empowerment that the model states should be built into any community development activity, whether with groups of interest and identity, or with communities of place.

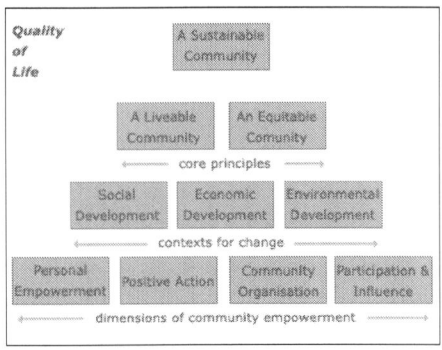

Figure 3: The ABCD Model

Source: Barr, A. and Hashagen, S. (2000) *The ABCD Handbook*, London: CDF (adapted from *proving and improving: a quality and impact toolkit for social enterprise*).

The centre of the diagram represents the context in which change takes place. Government and local government agencies, as well as companies and parts of the voluntary sector are responsible for policy, management and service delivery in social, economic and environmental development. CD requires them to engage with communities in accordance with the dimensions of community empowerment, in order to work collaboratively towards the outcomes of 'sustainability', or long-term viability of the community; 'livability', or community satisfaction; and 'equitability', or community safety.

The diagram offers a framework within which all stakeholders in the community development process can locate themselves, and identify the relationships which should be built to achieve change (Barr and Hashagen, 2000).

Chapter Three

3.0 Research Methodology

The Choice of Research Methodology

Research, according to the *Economic and Social Research Council* is the application of systematic techniques and methods in pursuit of answers to questions (ESRC online, 2009). The two generally defined types of research methodologies are those that use qualitative or quantitative techniques to collect and analyse data (ESRC Online material, 2009). A good researcher should explain how data was collected and evidence studied in order to meet the set aims and objectives of the study.

Qualitative research is the collection and analysis of information based on its quality, while quantitative research methodology is concerned with numbers and other things that are quantifiable (Flick, 2002). However in some cases, one methodology may not satisfy the needs of a research study; therefore requiring a combination of both methods, and/ or 'inductive strategies' (Flick, 2002: 2).

This study relies on literature review and case studies, both forms of qualitative research methodology. According to Robert Yin (2003) 'how' and 'why' questions are more explanatory and case studies are the preferred strategy to explain situations (Yin, 2003:1-6). This being a multi-method research, case studies will help explain how (or how not) PPP has contributed to community development in Rwanda. This study also reviews and analyses existing literature, relevant policy documents and academic material in an attempt to thoroughly answer the research question. Literature refers to a collection of books, documents, papers and historical records that deal with the same issues and that "respond to each other in the developing debates about a topic" (Fisher, 2007:86).

Literature on PPP in Rwanda is still lacking, but there are policy documents, political speeches, media reports and discussion papers that this study has analysed. Fisher argues that the important skill in literature review is the ability to condense large volumes of literature so that the essential views or arguments they contain can be presented in a small number of words (Fisher, 2007).

Efforts have also been made to correspond with Rwandan officials who are or have been involved with PPP development. The correspondences have largely been by electronic mail or telephone conversation.

According to Clifford (1997) qualitative research methodology is an approach that helps to draw some meaning out of a given situation.

This research methodology, according to Silverman (1994) and Miles and Hubermans (1994), is characterised by the following features:

- ❖ the research seeks to establish a holistic perspective of the situation
- ❖ the research is conducted in 'real life' day-to-day situations

- there is no single standardised way of collecting data
- the researcher uses small selective samples
- most analysis is done using words
- many interpretations of data are possible depending on the theoretical stance of the research
- the researcher may interact with the person being observed
- the researcher uses inductive reasoning
- the research is of low reliability but high validity
- no claims are made to generalise the findings (cited in Clifford, 1997:20).

Based on these features, this methodology is believed to satisfy the needs of this research. Three factors influenced the choice and use of this methodology:

Firstly, this study is concerned with drawing meaning out of available literature and from analysis of existing situation.

Secondly, there was the practical difficulties of travelling to Rwanda to conduct research, although the author has been a frequent traveller to the country which helped with direct observation and initial contacts; and

Thirdly, PPP is new in Rwanda; there was no historical data that would support some other research methodology.

Data Collection

Any research theory must be backed by data to explain it and help it have any meaning. A good researcher therefore must provide data to back up a theory or an assumption and must demonstrate where and how data was obtained.

Some of the methods used in qualitative research are interview, direct observation, literature review and examination and analysis of policy documents and historical records (Clifford, 1997).

Data for this study were collected through a variety of ways based on literature review and examination of document and policies. Data were obtained from Rwanda government sources, especially the ministries of finance, commerce, local government, education and Rwanda Development Board (RDB) as well as many other agencies dealing with economic, policy and development issues. Personal connections and contacts in these ministries and agencies were very helpful in this process. Information and contacts were also obtained from the Embassy of Rwanda (EoR) in London.

Further more, the researcher approached institutions that were targets of case studies such as Kigali Institute of Science and Technology and obtained permission to use online data and images of the institute. This study was also informed by daily newspapers reports, especially the New Times, Rwanda's only English language daily.

Online government sources, especially the President's and the Prime Minister's Offices; international organizations active in Rwanda's development process, private sector sources were also used in this study. Information from organizations such as the United Nations Development Programme, the World Bank, the International Monetary Fund, the UK's Department for International Development, were particularly useful.

The researcher also employed 'purposive/theoretical sampling' method (Clifford, 1997: 23), where various Rwandan officials dealing with PPP and related policy issues were approached through emails and telephone calls and requested to provide information on these issues. Respondents were assigned anonymous alphabetical identities to ensure their anonymity.

However, some officials who had promised to provide information withdrew their offer or simply did not respond as promised; one official explained that discussing this issue could lead to loss of job or even threats to personal safety (Respondent 'K')[3] . Some of these officials were considered highly informed in this area and their insight into this new concept will be missed in this study.

Data Validation and Administration

To ensure the validity of the data collected, the researcher made efforts to double check every information with a second source before it was deemed valid enough to be used in this study. Information supplied through email communication or telephone conservation was double-checked through relevant policy documents or by contacting another department or official with

---

[3] *Telephone Conversation dated August 13th, 2009*

related responsibilities. Semi-structured questions were used to give respondents an opportunity to comment on the topic without restrictions (Clifford, 1997). Low structured (open) approach was also used in certain circumstances, especially with telephone conversations. Table 1 below describes three approaches to interviews.

Highly structured	Semi-structured	Low structured
❖ structured questions ❖ fixed order/sequence ❖ data can be analysed numerically ❖ mostly used in quantitative research	❖ focused questions ❖ sequence of questioning may vary ❖ data transcribed into words ❖ mostly used in qualitative research	❖ open questions ❖ conversational approach-no prescribed sequence ❖ data transcribed into words ❖ mostly used in qualitative research

Table 1: approaches to interviews. *Source:* OLF (Clifford, 1997:41).

In terms of data administration, telephone conversations were transcribed and filed according to date of the conversation and the respondent's real identity alongside the assigned alphabetical identity. Email responses were similarly filed for reference purposes. This information cannot be used for any purpose other than this research study and shall be destroyed after use.

Ethical considerations

London Metropolitan University places a very high importance on ethical issues in any research. Every research undertaken at the University has to be approved by departmental Research Ethics Committee (REC), and this study received the approval of the Department of Applied Social Sciences' (DASS) REC.

Ethical issues in research are about the balance between protecting the rights of people you are dealing in your research, whilst at the same time pursuing your research interests. These include the right to privacy, safety, confidentiality and protection from manipulation or deceit (Clifford, 1997).

According to Fisher a researcher should not treat people unfairly or badly.

"You should not harm people, or use the information you discover in research to harm them, or allow it to be used to do harm" (Fisher, 2007:63). The researcher must ensure that participants in the research do so voluntarily without any form of coercion or deceit; that the participants give their informed consent and are clearly informed of all procedures and any risks involved, if any; that they are assured of confidentiality and anonymity; and that the research respects data protection laws (Trochim, 2006).

According to the University of York's *Code of Good Practice for Research*, ethical issues also arise from the basic principle that research activities should neither include practices which directly impose a risk of serious harm nor be indirectly dependent upon such practices. Serious harms include, for example, failure to respect the interests of human beings and damage to items of cultural value or the natural environment (University of York, 2006)

Bruce Berg argues that social scientists need to take utmost care because they "delve into the private social lives of other human beings" (Berg, 2001:39).

This research study was deemed to have no risk of harm to participants, and in line with and in respect of these ethical considerations; the researcher drafted an explanatory statement as well as a consent form (*Appendix A*). The statement explains the purpose of the research and the procedures that are used in the research. It also explains that participation is voluntary and assures the participants that all their rights will be respected in accordance with the University ethical rules and the data protection laws of the United Kingdom. The statement and consent form were approved by the University and were used in every information request or any request for participation in this research. Participants were also assured the right to withdraw their consent at any point without being required to give any reasons and to reserve their right to retract any information provided.

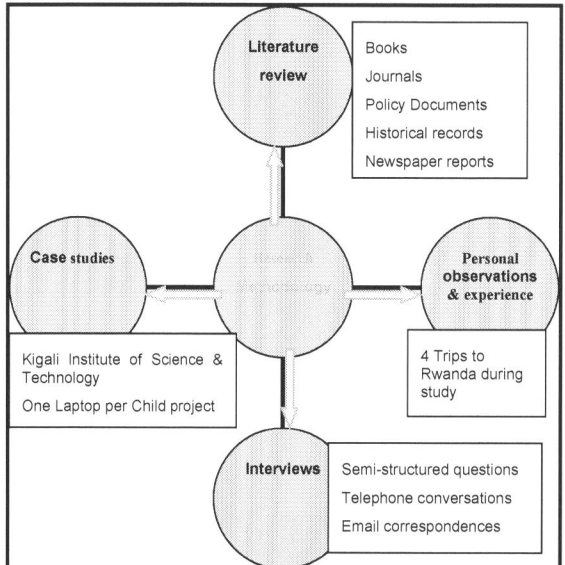

Figure 4: Research Methods used in this study
Source: Author

This study admits to the limitations in fully employing the chosen research methods. There were limitations caused by distance and inadequate resources, for instance to conduct structured interviews or surveys. If not for these limitations, the researcher would have wished to spend time in Rwanda, conduct structured interviews with both public and private sector leaders; carry out surveys and examine more cases where PPP has been used or attempted, especially in energy and telecommunication sectors, where the government has had a few quarrels with international investors, Terracom and Dane Associates (De Lorenzo, 2008).

Both case studies in this study relied on literature review especially of policy documents, online material and newspaper reports; correspondence with few officials and direct observation during previous visits to Rwanda. This falls short of multiple sources of evidence normally recommended for case studies, which allows the researcher to address a broader range of issues (Yin, 2003).

It is my belief that probably the conclusions of this study would have been more convincing and accurate was it to be based on different sources of information, and the chosen research methods were used exhaustively. Yin, however, recommends as well, that if the researcher does not fulfil the prerequisites of multiple sources of evidence, it is better to rely on a single or a few sources than use multiple sources improperly (Yin, 2003).

Furthermore, some officials whose insights would have enriched this study withdrew their co-operation for various reasons; others did not respond to my enquiries.

In spite of these challenges, however, this study made good use of chosen research methods in prevailing circumstances and one can argue that its findings and conclusions represent a better outcome in this situation.

Chapter Four

4.0 Analysis and Case Studies

Data Analysis Approach

This study follows an interpretative data analysis approach, with a phenomenological bent (Berg, 2001). In this approach, according to Berg, researchers treat social actions and human activity as text or a collection of symbols expressing layers of meaning. This allows researchers to transcribe interviews and observational data into written text for analysis and how one interprets the text depends on the theoretical orientation adopted by the researcher. With a phenomenological orientation, the researcher avoids condensing data by various sorting or coding methods, but instead attempts to capture the essence of the information analysed (Berg, 2001).

The above author argues that this approach "provides a means for discovering the practical understanding of meanings and actions" (Berg, 2001:239). In applying this approach, this study attempts to unpack the meaning of and provide understanding of policies, actions and information from various sources. On the other hand, considering the fact that this study involves case studies, it has applied theoretical propositions and content analysis strategies to analyse and learn lessons from verbatim and documentary texts (Yin, 2003). Based on the propositions that shaped this research design and data collection plan, this study gives priority to the relevant analytic strategies to arrive at relevant recommendations and conclusions.

PPP in Rwanda: A brief overview

In Rwanda PPP is part of the National Public Investment Policy (NPIP) and is still a new concept under development.

President Paul Kagame fired the first shot in the country's battle to adopt PPP when at an investment conference in Kigali in 2003 he... reiterated his government's commitment to what he called "the ability to learn and innovate fast, and the capacity to enhance competitiveness through smart partnership" (Kagame, 2003). Then and now, the President continues to provide strong political backing to this new initiative.

Kagame told a conference in Germany recently:

"....we have to realize that we cannot tackle these tasks alone and must turn to the private sector to bring in the required finance, technology and skills" (Kagame, 2009).

A military general and a former rebel leader, who allegedly is the only head of state in the world to have trained in both United States and Cuba (Kinzer, 2008), the Rwandan leader has surprised many observers and turned out to be a shrewd economic reformer (Bindra, 2009), 'a master of marketing' (The Adams, 2009) and has been a major influence behind Rwanda's political and economic fortunes for the last (nearly) two decades. With Tony Blair as President Kagame's advisor, no surprise that Rwanda is taking on the 'New Public Sector Management" concept with the same zeal as "New Labour" did after assuming power in Britain in 1997(Corry, D., in Ghobadian, *et al*, eds., 2004).

Top Rwandan officials have pronounced themselves in favour of PPP, although the concept is barely known to the general public, and there is lingering suspicion among private sector operators that public sector officials act against or try to sabotage PPP initiatives (Kakimba, 2009).

The Prime Minister Bernard Makuza is quoted to have told a meeting of Rwandan officials and external donors (known in Rwanda as "development partners") in November 2008 that there was need to venture into innovations that will ensure long term sustainable development is achieved....and to build stronger collaboration between the government and the private sector working together on public-private partnerships.

(Kimenyi, 2008).

PPPs will be pivotal in supporting some of the country's big infrastructural projects that include the Dar es Salaam –Kigali railway, the Kampala-Kigali oil pipeline and the soon-to-be-constructed International Airport, the country's finance and economic planning minister James Musoni is quoted to have told the same meeting. Rwanda's infrastructure minister Linda Bihire is also banking on PPP for the delivery of the country's biggest project ever, the $US4bn railway line linking Rwanda and Tanzania. She is quoted to have said that the project is expected to be realised through PPP (Kimenyi, 2008).

Many scholars and experts agree with the optimism Rwandan officials have in PPP. As a post-conflict country, Rwanda must look at new innovative ways to rebuild her infrastructure and to achieve long term development objectives. In *Public-Private Partnerships in State-Building and Recovery from Conflict,* John Bray (2006) asserts that collaboration between government and business is especially important in states that are recovering from conflict.

Graeme *et al* (in Osborne, 20004: 202-203) have argued that PPPs have become a tool for providing public services and developing a civil society in post-communist countries, and a mechanism for combating social exclusion and enhancing community development under European Union policy.

One of the countries whose development model Rwanda is emulating is South Korea, where PPP has played a pivotal role in the country's infrastructure development. South Korea is heavily involved in Rwanda, advising the government on development strategy (KOICA/KDS, 2009) and delivering some of the country's infrastructure projects such as the 2300-kilometer-$40 million fibre optic broadband cable, and the $70 million wireless broadband network known as "Kigali Metropolitan Area Network" according to the country's daily the New Times. Information technology minister Romain Murenzi believes the partnership with KT (Korea Telecom) is helping to transform Rwanda into a continental ICT hub (Kagire, 2009; Tong-hyung, 2009).

The Organisation for Economic Co-operation & Development (OECD) reports that as of August 2006, Korea had 64 projects under operation, 76 under construction, 35 preparing to construct, 53 under negotiations and 32 under review (Park, 2006, quoted in OECD, 2008). South Korea is among Asian countries that were referred to as "developmental states" in 1970s. Defined as the " seamless web of political, bureaucratic, and moneyed influences that structures economic life in capitalist Northeast Asia" developmental states pursued aggressive economic development and growth, through a system in which "private ownership" was combined "with state guidance" (Woo-Cumings, ed.,1999:1-2). According to Mark Beeson (2003), a developmental state is one that influences the direction and pace of economic development by directly intervening in the development process, rather than just relying on market forces to allocate economic resources.

Rwandan policymakers will be encouraged by these examples and the South Koreans will encourage Rwanda to follow a similar route. Whether Rwanda will become the first "developmental state" in Africa is a question that will be answered by history.

Rwanda is also a member of the East African Community (EAC), which is committed to developing what it calls "strategic partnerships" and "tapping more effectively sources of financing from the private sector through Public Private Partnerships" (EAC Development Strategy, 2006:12). The EAC is the regional grouping of five countries known as 'Partner States' of Burundi, Kenya, Rwanda, Tanzania and Uganda.

PPP Framework in Rwanda

Although Rwandan top officials support PPP, apparently there is a thin presence of a coherent PPP framework to guide its implementation on the ground. Apart from mention of PPP in the Country's National Public Investment Policy (NPIP), and 'other bits and pieces here and there" as one Rwandan official put it, (*Respondent* 'P', 2009)[4] there is no PPP legislation and not yet detailed procedures to guide public officials on how to implement this initiative, nor is there any detailed framework on how to work with the private sector with regard to PPP, but officials insist these policies and procedures are all in the pipeline. Another official stated that "at the moment laws in each individual sector such as mining, energy, telecom, serve as guidelines to PPPs" (*Respondent* 'A', 2009)[5], confirming respondent P's view.

The NPIP acknowledges that management of "potential PPPs has so far been hitherto scattered within various Ministries or Government institutions" (NPIP, 2009:22). One official hinted this lack of guidelines is making it very difficult to conclude PPP deals, saying "there is no general rule or any other guideline, which makes it very difficult to conclude a deal in that area" (Respondent 'A', 2009)[6]. According to this official, a draft law on private financed infrastructure projects has remained a draft for the last 2 years "and I have no idea when it might be looked at again".

President Kagame acknowledged lack of, and promised development of PPP framework while addressing a conference in Germany recently, saying it was essential to strengthening the framework for Public Private Partnership in Rwanda for sustainable economic growth and development, and to

---

[4] Respondent P, telephone conversation with the researcher, dated August 8th, 2009

[5] Respondent A, email communication dated July 18th, 2009

[6] Respondent A, ibid

continue to reform the way government works with private investors (Kagame, 2009).

The NPIP provides that:

"private investment, including Public Private Partnership... can play a pivotal role in supporting the accelerated delivery of strategic national infrastructure, yield long term value for money and ensure quality public services without jeopardizing debt sustainability" (NPIP, 2009:4). The NPIP also commits the Rwandan government to the need to maximize efficiency of public investment, promote investment in new and innovative ways "including promotion and adoption of Public Private Partnerships" (NPIP, 2009:7). It adds that a systematic and programmed application of PPP would result in better allocation and utilization of public funds and ensure budgetary sustainability; efficient and good quality public infrastructure, economic growth and increased foreign direct investment; transfer of risks to the party best able to control and manage them; and maximize benefits of private sector efficiency, expertise, flexibility and innovation.

In summary, provision of quality public services efficiently and effectively, value for money, attracting private sector expertise and innovation, and sustainable debt/budget management, are some of the drivers of PPP policy in Rwanda, very much like in many other countries. The government says it considers PPP as "one of the primary triggers of growth " (NPIP,2009:8); "an important building block for investment" (NPIP, 2009:9); and states that further reforms are needed to guarantee that public investment constitutes a catalyst of, and a complement to, private investment. NPIP is also aligned to country's poverty reduction strategy (EDPRS).

The NPIP requires the private sector partner to assume "significant technical, financial, and operational risk" (NPIP, 2009:14); and to contribute at least 30% equity finance for its share of investment costs. It promises the development of a comprehensive PPP framework, addressing issues such as pre-conditions and procedures for PPP, delivery models, management and implementation responsibilities in line ministries, and rules and regulations; and a PPP implementation manual covering all stages from project inception to completion. A PPP Unit is envisaged, which, in close collaboration with line ministries and other stakeholders, will be responsible to conceptualize, design and package complex PPP and joint venture transactions; and to provide integrated advisory services to responsible line ministries and other stakeholders.

The process of staffing the PPP Unit has started, with the Ministry of Finance hiring a foreign consultant and issuing a recruitment notice for PPP secretariat in July 2009. Vacancies advertised include that of PPP Unit coordinator, a senior financial analyst, a legal & procurement specialist, and a logistics, capacity building and administration officer (Respondent 'M', 2009)[7].

PPP is a highly complex concept even in developed countries with high

---

[7] Minecofin, Recruitment Notice for the PPP Secretariat, email dated, August 4th, 2009

managerial skills. In Rwanda, like in many other developing countries the managerial capacity to handle such a complex initiative will continue to be a challenge. High skilled managers are needed to prepare winning PPP projects, negotiate with private sector entities and deal with contractual issues arising out of PPP (Davies, 2008).

The NPIP provides for capacity building, in both the public and private sectors, by first sourcing international experts, who are expected to pass on knowledge to local firms. International advisors and local consulting firms are encouraged to form consortia and share experiences and expertise as a way to develop local capacity. The government promises appropriate incentive schemes to facilitate partnerships between local and international firms.

There is no doubt that the NPIP constitutes a very strong political commitment by the Rwandan government to the promotion and application of PPP principles, but policy does not hold the same strength as a law. An initiative as complex as PPP cannot and should not be practised on the basis of policy alone. What is needed is a strong legislative backing of PPP and detailed step-by-step guidelines on how public bodies will design, negotiate and implement PPP projects. This will provide stability in the PPP market and give confidence to reputable international firms to participate in Rwanda's PPP, hence further helping it to develop to international standards.

PPP case studies in Rwanda's education sector

Since 1994 the Rwandan government has been reforming the country's education system based on the concept of meritocracy rather than favouritism that had characterised the previous system of education in the country. The aim of the new system, according to the government, is to create a highly skilled and productive workforce that will drive Rwanda towards industrialization and development in the years to come (*Achievements of the government National Unity*, 2009). The reforms include the removal of an ethnic quota system for entry into schools and universities, which was making access to education limited for sections of the population, the setting up of a national examination board to ensure fairness, transparency and uniformity of standards and promoting education of the girl child. Other bodies and agencies established to develop and facilitate access to quality education include the National Curriculum Development Centre (NCDC), Students Financing Agency of Rwanda (SFAR), the National Commission for UNESCO, the National Council for Higher Education (NCHE), the Teachers' Service Commission (TSC), and the Inspectorate General for Education (*Ministry of Education, 2009*).

According to Rwanda's *Education Strategic Plan*, the four priorities are fee-free education, rectification of gender-based disparities in education, promoting trilingualism, fighting HIV/AIDS and putting emphasis on science & technology (*Ministry of education strategic plan, 2006*).

These reforms have enabled the development of several education institutions, some private, others public under partnership with other stakeholders. The case study will focus on two partnerships: Kigali Institute of Science and Technology (KIST), which was established in collaboration with United Nations Development Programme (UNDP) and the German Agency for Technical Co-operation (GTZ), and One Laptop per Child (OLPC), which aims to avail laptop computers to Rwandan children, in partnership with the OLPC organisation (itnewsafrica, 2009). The analysis of these case studies will show how partnership in education has the potential to advance community development in a poor country like Rwanda. By contribution to community development, this study wants to examine whether these partnerships are creating or leading to the creation of tools that empower the poor people and lead to improvement in their lives.

Case Study 1: Kigali Institute of Science and Technology (KIST)

KIST was founded in 1997, 3 years after the Genocide that killed nearly a million people and destroyed the country's education and other infrastructure. A product of a partnership between the government of Rwanda (GoR), United Nations Development Programme (UNDP) and German Agency for Technical Co-operation (GTZ), the institute was founded with the aim of providing science and technology education in Rwanda and to produce technicians and scientists of "high calibre". This was part of the new Rwandan government's mission of building a strong post-Genocide human resource base. The initial funding for the institute came from a UNDP core funding and a UNDP Trust Fund provided by the governments of Japan and the Netherlands. Although after the genocide Rwanda was a basket case in need of charity, GoR provided the land and buildings, which at that time housed a military college (*Appendix B*), and GoR was involved in the management of the project.

KIST's Contribution to Community Development in Rwanda

The institute has established a Centre for Innovation and Technology Transfer (CITT), under a partnership arrangement between GoR and the UK's Department for International Development (DFID). CITT's mission is to use applied research to produce environmentally friendly and appropriate technological innovations, which can be used by rural communities. Over 90% of Rwandan population is rural-based, and this will take technology solutions to the rural community.

CITT says its objective is to spearhead the transformation of the social economic conditions of the Rwandan rural and peri-urban communities, through increased application of appropriate technologies.

After seven years of existence (2002-2009), CITT says it has been able to develop the following appropriate technologies that benefit the community:

- ❖ Waste water management and production of Biogas for schools, households and prisons, which, according to CITT has led to tremendous saving on fuel wood consumption, hence minimising deforestation and arresting creeping desertification

Figure 5: Construction of biogas digester designed by KIST

Source: www.kist.ac.rw, *used with kind permission of the Rector of KIST*

- ❖ Fuel efficient community cooking stoves to address the problem of an acute shortage of fuel energy for cooking in institutions and in households
- ❖ Other energy saving technologies have also been developed including home solar system, kerosene shower, bread oven etc.
- ❖ Low cost housing, which is aimed at addressing high cost of construction, especially among low income earners
- ❖ Rainwater harvesting and storage
- ❖ Food storage (Storage bin, Maize storage crib)
- ❖ Agriculture technologies (Treadle pump, Maize Sheller, Rice thresher, potato peeler, tomato pulper, et cetera)
- ❖ Water supply (hand pump used to draw water from underground tank)

CITT says also provides capacity building training in:

- ❖ Biogas plants construction.
- ❖ Environmental conservation through urns construction in

> households.
> - ❖ Women's associations in food processing technologies and business skills[8].
>
> Rwanda has also embarked on establishing 'community telecentres' throughout the countryside, in partnership with Cisco Networking Academy, to help rural communities' access to information technology solutions (Kagire, 2009) such as e-health and market information for their produce. KIST has been producing IT graduates every year and one can assume that these graduates are playing a critical role in this exercise.
>
> ***Case Study 2: One Laptop per Child Project***
>
> In 2007 Rwanda entered a partnership with the One Laptop per Child (OLPC) organisation to bring computer literacy to primary school students in the country as part of preparing the country for medium income economy envisioned by the year 2020. In a country where only 4% of schools have access to electricity, it looked like a distortion of priorities.
>
> But since the project was launched 20,000 OX laptop computers have already been distributed to schools and the government plans to import 100,000 more laptops in 2009 (Kwizera, 2009) and by May 2009,120,000 laptops were

---

[8] *Source:* http://www.kist.ac.rw/about/about.html; http://www.kist.ac.rw/centers/citt.html, accessed 30. 06.09.

reported as the target for the year (Gahigi, 2009). OLPC reported that the Rwandan government has committed 2.2 million primary school children to have laptop computers by the year 2012 (OLPC.ORG, 2009)

In June 2009, the OLPC organisation launched a Global Centre of Excellence in Laptops and Learning, in Rwanda, marking the success registered by the project so far (OLPC.ORG, 2009). A team of expatriate engineers, known as OLPCCorps have been working alongside their Rwandan counterparts to train students and ensure the project's success.

OLPC founder Nicholas Negroponte, said the project has experienced great success with support from both the government (top down) as well as from grassroots (bottom up). "The partnership with Rwanda represents a substantial commitment by both OLPC and Rwanda to bring learning to the grassroots and country level, which is exactly where it should be", according to an OLPC report (OLPC.ORG, 2009).

The report quoted Theoneste Mutsindashyaka, Rwandan Minister of State in charge of Primary and Secondary Education as saying, "the new Center will strengthen the local team working on OLPC rollout in Rwanda, and further support it in terms of capacity development, technology acquisition and innovation, building networks of laptops, maintenance, and content development."

Contribution to Community Development

To what extent OLPC will contribute to community development is too early to determine, since the project is still in its infancy. However, it is envisaged that it will sharpen the pupils' research skills at a young age, encourage discovery and stimulate innovativeness and creative thinking, according to project coordinator, Richard Niyonkuru (Gahigi, 2009). Niyonkuru argues that it will empower the pupils to assume a central position in their own learning as opposed to teachers being custodians of knowledge.

The importance of exposing young minds to such learning tools and the impact that will have on their communities in a poor country like Rwanda, also cannot be underestimated.

In a decade or so, when these kids have became computer wizards, life might never be the same for them, their families and their communities. The transformative power of information and Communications Technology (ICT) may lead to transformation of Rwandan communities, like it has done elsewhere. This could mark the beginning of community empowerment, hence community development.

Conclusion

As noted elsewhere in this study, PPP is still a new concept, and these two case studies are the closest to PPP Rwanda has had in the education sector. In most developing countries like Rwanda, most PPP projects will probably take this shape, with involvement of 'development partners' before proper business PPP projects emerge. So Rwanda's example may provide an insight into PPP trend in developing countries.

Nonetheless this study concludes that these partnerships are very important in supporting community development initiatives in Rwanda and should be promoted in other developing countries.

This study concludes that whereas PPP has no yet had any serious impact on community development in Rwanda, the potential is there and the beginning is very promising.

CHAPTER FIVE:
5.0 Conclusion

This study set out to investigate the impact of PPP on community development in Rwanda. It looked at the arguments for and against PPP, its history and spectrum, various models, weaknesses and keys to success or failure of PPP.

Further more, it looked at a brief overview of PPP in Rwanda, analysed the country's PPP policy and assessed two case studies in the education sector. The study carried out a comparative analysis of PPP and community development, and community development vs. economic growth.

The study found that PPP is a very new concept in Rwanda, still evolving and will continue to evolve. Though politicians and top leaders are in favour PPP, its presence on the ground in terms of legislation, implementation procedures and guidelines is very thin. What should be of great concern to proponents of PPP and policy makers in Rwanda is that it is not yet well understood both in the public and private sectors. There is suspicion by some in the private sector that some officials in the public sector could be hostile to PPP, either because they don't understand it or they see it as a threat to their own positions.

So there is a need to design strategies to counter this hostility and to educate the public and private sector officials about the advantages of PPP and how it works. The success of PPP depends very much on the ability of these two sectors working together, as to good legislation, policies and commitment from the top echelons of the government.

Top politicians are solidly behind PPP and economic dynamics and international trends make it the most favoured way forward in infrastructure development in Rwanda. However, this study found a serious threat to the development of PPP in Rwanda, in the form of corruption, poor management practices and lack of capacity in both public and private sectors. There is no doubt that the Rwandan government is committed to fighting corruption in public service, but reports continue to show its existence in crucial public sector organisations, like the judiciary, police and procurement agencies. This study found that Rwanda still has a long way to go in building proper PPP frameworks, and a lot needs to be done to get there. The country needs a strong PPP legislation, procedures and guidelines that will attract international players in the PPP market. PPP is very complex and will take time for both the public and private sectors to learn and understand it; but awareness programmes need to be intensified for this process to move faster.

In terms of PPP's impact on community development, this study found this very difficult to assess due to the fact that PPP has no track record in the country. There was no baseline data on which to base the assessment apart from a few achievements registered by Kigali Institute of Science and Technology. Instead the study makes recommendations on how PPP could contribute to community development. Even the case studies undertaken didn't provide much evidence, and this study asserts that these were not actually typical PPP. They hardly fit into the typical PPP models, but they point to a very interesting trend in developing countries, where governments and 'development partners' work together to achieve common development objectives.

The first case study, Kigali Institute of Science and Technology (KIST) was conceived as development assistance to post-genocide Rwanda, at a time when Rwanda was still basket case. That was long before the PPP idea was conceived. This study found that out of this gesture of charity a great institution was born, which has made tremendous contribution to Rwanda's skills development. KIST has produced some of the best engineers and technicians that are spearheading the country's technological revolution and powering economic development. KIST has also researched and put on the market innovative products and initiatives that are changing ordinary people's lives. For this reason, this study concludes that KIST has made a big impact on community development and in the transformation of Rwanda.

The second case study, One Laptop per Child project (OLPC) is about a year old and there is no baseline data on which to assess its impact. This is also not your typical PPP. However the author decided to take this as case study because it is revolutionary in its intent. The impact of empowering young people with modern technology skills can only be imagined now, but it should not be underestimated. Elsewhere Information and Communication Technology (ICT) has transformed many societies beyond recognition in just one generation. The author believes that, through these young children that are being exposed to ICT early in life, this transformative power of technology is coming to Rwanda. In a decade when these kids have became computer wizards, life might never be the same for them, their families and their communities. This, together with other policies in the pipeline such as EDPRS, NPIP and Vision 2020, has the power to change the way things are done in Rwanda and to change the country beyond recognition.

It will transform agriculture, the mainstay of most Rwandans; it will open Rwanda up to the rest of the world in real terms, and open world markets for Rwandan products; it will empower people and communities; it will change social interactions; it will transform power relations; it will change political and economic systems and institutions-it will lead to social and economic transformation. It will bring community development closer than ever to the people of Rwanda!

The only caveat being that Rwanda continues to enjoy uninterrupted stability and its leadership continues to be visionary and steadfastly anti-corruption; hence bucking the trend in Africa.

Finally this study rejects the notion that PPP is only for big, complex projects, for the sole purpose of promoting "economic growth". This study posits that PPP can also be used for small local community projects that have the power to reach the lowest pockets of poverty. This study argues that PPP can and should be used for poverty reduction and community development initiatives, and for rural development in Rwanda and Africa. Investors must be enticed to venture into rural development. Governments must channel public money into this and build partnerships with business to tackle rural poverty. In the long term, it will make business sense when formerly poverty-stricken and marginalised communities join the formal economy and become consumers of goods and services. "By investing in people and the environment, businesses also ensure their own commercial success" according to GTZ (GTZ, Online, 2009).

Chapter Six

6.0 References and Appendices

References:

Abel-Smith, B. (1976) *Value for Money in Health Services*, London: Heinemann

Adams, T. (2009) *Starbucks founder spreads gospel of hope in Rwanda* {online} The Observer19th July 2009. Available at: http://www.guardian.co.uk/environment/2009/jul/19/starbucks-howard-schultz-fairtrade {accessed 20/07/09}.

Amanpour, C. (2008) *Woman opens heart to man who slaughtered her family* {online}, CNN, 15th May 2008. Available at: http://edition.cnn.com/WORLD/africa/05/15/amanpour.rwanda/index.html {accessed 24/08/09}.

Barr, A., and Hashagen, S. (2000), *ABCD Handbook,* London: Community Development Foundation (CDF)

Beeson, M. (2003) *The rise and fall (?) of the developmental state: the vicissitudes and implications of East Asian interventionism* {online}, available at: http://espace.library.uq.ed.au/eserv/uq:10916/mb-ds-03.pdf {accessed 12/08/09}.

Berg, B.L. (2001) *Qualitative Research Methods for the Social Sciences* (4th edn.), Boston: Allyn & Bacon

Bindra, S. (2009) *Take-home lessons from tiny Rwanda* {online}, The Nation Media Group, June13th, 2009. Available at:

http://www.nation.co.ke/oped/Opinion/-/440808/610350/-/item/1/-/188yg2/-/inde x.html {accessed 15/06/09}.

Bray, J. (2006) *Public Private Partnerships in State-Building and Recovery from Conflict*, London: Chatham House.

British Columbia, Ministry of Municipal Affairs (1999) *Public Private Partnership: A Guide for Local Government* (online) available at:http://www.cd.gov.bc.ca/lgd/policy research/library/public private partners hips.pdfand http://www.pppcouncil.ca {accessed 23/06/09}.

Brittan, S. (2001) *Public Private Partnerships: A temporary landmark for the third way*, Winchester, 13.11.01 {n.p}

Broomes, V. (2009) *'Triple wins' from Foreign Direct Investment*, London: CPSU

Canadian Council for Public-Private Partnerships: {n.d} *Definitions* {online}, available at: http://www.pppcouncil.ca/aboutPPP definition.asp {accessed 22/06/09}.

Chang, C. V. (2006) *Privatization and Development: Theory, Policy and Evidence*, Hampshire: Ashgate Publishing Ltd.

CHRI (2009) *Rwanda's Application for Membership of the Commonwealth: Report of a mission of the Commonwealth Human Rights Initiative*, May 2009: New Delhi/London: CHRI

Clifford, C. (1997) *Qualitative Research Methodology in Nursing and Healthcare*, London: Open Learning Foundation

Collin, S., and Hanson, L. (2000) *The propensity, persistence and performance of public- private partnerships in Sweden*, in Osborne, S.P. ed.,

(2000) *Public-Private Partnerships: Theory and Practice in International Perspective*, London: Routledge

Corry, D. (2004) *New Labour and PPPs*, in Ghobadian, A., Gallear, D., O'Regan, N., and Viney, H. (2004) Public-Private Partnerships: Policy and Experience, Hampshire: Palgrave Macmillan

Davie, J. (2008) presentation at *The Business Futures Forum: The Future of PPP in Africa*, London Metropolitan Business School, 02/12/08

De Lorenzo, M. (2008) *The Rwandan Paradox: Is Rwanda a model for an Africa beyond Aid?* January 1, 2008, American Enterprise institute for Public Policy Research (online). Available at: http://www.aei.org/article/27476 , {accessed 28/08/09}.

Department for Communities and Local Government (2007): *The Community Development Challenge,* London: Crown Copyright

EAC (2006) *Development Strategy 2006-2010 {online}*, available at: http://www.eac.int/about-eac/strategic-partnerships.html; http://infrastructure.eac.int {accessed 06/07/09}.

EIB (2004) *The EIB's role in Public-Private Partnerships {online},* available at http://eib.org/projects/publications/the-eibs-role-in-public-private-partnerships-ppps-htm?lang=en {accessed 29/07/09}.

ESRC, (2009) *Research Methods {online}.* Available at: http://www.esrcsocietytoday.ac.uk/ESRCInfoCentre/research/ResearchMethods/ {accessed 22/07/09}.

EU (2008) *EU Election Observation Mission, Kenya, 27 December 2007: Final Report on the General Elections, April 3rd, 2008.*

Falconer, P.K., and McLaughlin (2000) *Public-private partnerships and the 'New Labour' Government in Britain*, in Osborne, S.P. ed., (2000) *Public-Private Partnerships: Theory and Practice in International Perspective*, London: Routledge

Farlam, P. (2005) *Working Together: Assessing Public Private Partnership in Africa*, Nepad Policy Focus Series, Johannesburg: The South African Institute of International Affairs

Faulkner, K (2004) *Public Private Partnerships*, in Ghobadian, A., Gallear, D., O'Regan, N., and Viney, H., eds. (2004) *Public Private Partnerships: Policy and Experience*, Hampshire: Palgrave Macmillan

Fisher, C. (2007) *Researching and Writing a Dissertation: A Guide Book for Business Students* (2nd ed.), London: Pearson Education

Flick, U. (2002) *An Introduction to Qualitative Research* (2nd ed.), London: Sage Publications Ltd

Gahigi, M. (2009) *When the school curriculum goes digital*, The New Times {online} July 30th, 2009. Available at: http://www.newtimes.co.rw/index.php?issue=13972&article=18117 {accessed 30/07/09}.

Gatete, C. (2009), Ambassador of the Republic of Rwanda, speech during Rwanda Liberation Day celebration, London, July 4th, 2009.

Ghobadian, A., Gallear, D., O'Regan, N., and Viney, H., (eds.) (2004) *Public Private Partnerships: Policy and Experience*, Hampshire: Palgrave Macmillan

Gilchrist, A., with Rauf, T. (2006) *Community Development and Networking*, London: CDF

GoR (2009) *Achievements of the government of National Unity* {online} available at: http://www.gov.rw/government/government.html {accessed 10/07/09}.

GoR, Cabinet Meeting (2009) *Itangazo Ry'ibyemezo By'Inama Y'Abaminisitiri Yateraniye Muri Village Urugwiro Kuwa 07/08/09* {online}. Available at: http://www.gov.rw/news.php?id_article=78 {accessed 10/08/09}.

Gosling, T. ed. (2004): *3 STEPS FORWARD, 2 STEPS BACK: Reforming PPP Policy*, London: IPPR

GTZ (2009) *Public Private Partnership,* GTZ Centre for Cooperation the Private Sector {online} available at: http://south-africa.german-development-cooperation.org/topic/public-private-partnership {accessed 13/08/09}.

Hamilton, G. (2008) *Good Governance in Public-Private Partnerships*, presentation at UNECE conference, Geneva 18-19 September 2008.

HM Treasury (2000) *Public Private Partnerships: The Government's Approach*, London: The Stationery Office

HMSO (1998) *Better Quality Services: A handbook on creating PPPs through market testing and contracting out*, London: Crown Copyright

Huxman, C. and Vangen, S. (2000) *what makes partnerships work?* In Osborne, S.P. ed., (2000) *Public-Private Partnerships: Theory and Practice in International Perspective*, London: Routledge

IMF (2004) *Public-Private Partnerships* {online}. Available at http://www.imf.org/external/np/fad/2004/pifp/eng/031204.pdf {accessed 11/07/09}.

ITafricanews (2009) *One Laptop per Child Initiative Launched in Africa*, {online} March 19, 2009. Available at: http://www.itnewsafrica.com/?p=2413 {accessed 13/07/09}.

Kagame, P. (2003) *Keynote address to the Rwanda Investment Conference*, 12 04. 2003 {online}. Available at: http://www.gov.rw/government/president/speeches/index.html {accessed 28/11/ 2008}.

Kagame, P. (2006) In a Speech to the Rwandan Community in London, the Rwandan president said he has no apologies for being over-ambitious, London, October 6, 2006.

Kagame, P. (2008) speech at: *Africa and Rwanda: From Crisis to Socio-economic Development* conference 22nd May, 2008, Singapore: National University of Singapore

Kagame, P. (2009) *Interview by Fareed Zacharia on GPS programme*, CNN, July 19th, 2009, 20:00hrs

Kagame, P. (2009) *Remarks at dinner hosted by Altira Group and German Business Community* {online} Berlin April, 24th, 2009. Available at: http://www.presidency.gov.rw {accessed 15/06/09}.

Kagire, E. (2009) *KT opens regional office in Rwanda*, The New Times {online} May 22nd 2009. Available at: http://www.newtimes.co.rw/index.php?issue=13903&article=15934 {accessed 22/06/09}.

Kagire, E. (2009) *RDB-IT Cisco to setup academies in rural areas,* The New Times {online} July 24th, 2009. Available at:

http://www.newtimes.co.rw/index.php?issue=13966&article=17899 {accessed 24/07/2009}.

Kakimba, M. (2009) *Senate, PSF table flaw in PPP framework*, The New Times {online}, May 5th, 2009. Available at: http://www.newtimes.co.rw/index.php?issue=13939&email&article=1596&week=19 {accessed 08/05/09}.

Kasasira, R. & Bareebe, G. (2009) *Museveni disowns Entebbe airport deal*, The Daily Monitor {online} July 28th, 2009. Available at: http://www.monitor.co.ug/artman/publish/news/Museveni_disowns_Entebbe_airport_deal_88780.shtml {accessed 03/08/09}.

Kasasira, R. (2009) *Were we almost ripped off in the airport?* The Monitor [online} August 2nd, 2009. Available at: http://www.monitor.co.ug/artman/publish/inside_politics/Were_we_almost_ripped_off_in_the_airport_deal_88699.shtml {accessed 03/08/09}.

Kavuma, R.M (2006) *Uganda & Millennium Goals,* The Weekly Observer {online} April 13-19, 2006. Available at: http://www.observer.ug/docs/MDGs.pdf {accessed 22/07/2009}.

Kayumba, C. (2008) *Rwanda must tolerate bad news and spare the messengers*, The Monitor {online} January 2nd, 2008. Available at: http://www.monitor.co.ug/artman/publish/features/rwaanda_must_tolerate_bad_news_and_spare_the_messenger.shtml {accessed 19/08/09}.

Kimanuka, O. (2008) *Sub-Saharan Africa's Development Challenges: A Case Study of Rwanda's Post-Genocide Experience*, New York: Palgrave Macmillan.

Kimenyi, F. (2008) *Premier calls for inclusion of LDCs in financial crisis fight*, The New Times, November, 28th, 2008, p1.

Kimenyi, F. (2009) *Consult Africa, Kagame tells G-8*, The New Times {online} July 7th, 2009 Available at:

http://www.newtimes.co.rw/index.php?issue=13949&article=17256 {accessed 7/07/2009}.

Kimenyi, F. (2008) *Development partners' meeting starts today: public private partnership top on agenda*, The New Times, 27th, November 2008, p.1.

Kimenyi, F. (2008) *Multi-billion dollar railway project to kick off next year,* The New Times {online}, 11th November 2008, p.1.

Kinzer, S. (2008) *A Thousand Hills: Rwanda's Rebirth and the Man Who Dreamed it,* New York: John Wiley & Sons.

KOICA/KDS (2009) *Building Development Capacity of Strategic Areas in Rwanda*, final report, May 2009, Kigali: Office of the President, Strategy & Policy Unit.

Kwizera, C. (2009) *Rwanda: OLPC - 100,000 Computers to Be Imported This Year,* The New Times {online}, Jan. 8th, 2009. Available at:

http://allafrica.com/stories/200901080184.html {accessed 13/07/09}.

Lacy, S. (2009) *How to Cross the Digital Divide, Rwanda – Style*, The Washington Post {online} June 24th, 2009. Available at:

http://www.washingtonpost.com/wp-dyn/content/article/2009/06/24/AR2009062401533_pf.html {accessed 27/06/09}.

Ledwith, M. (2005): *COMMUNITY DEVELOPMENT: A critical approach,*

Bristol: The Policy Press

Lewis, W. A., (1976) *The Theory of Economic Growth*, London: George Allen & Unwin Ltd.

Link, A.N (2006) *Public/Private Partnerships: Innovative Strategies and Policy Alternatives*, New York: Springer Science + Media

Lissauer, R., Robinson, P. eds. (2000) *A learning process: Public-Private Partnerships in Education*, London: IPPR.

Little, I.M.D (1982) *Development: Theory, Policy and International Relations*, New York: Basic Books.

MINECOFIN, (2007) *Press Release: Day One of DPM (Development Partners' Meeting) Sees Launch of Major Development Strategy for Rwanda: The EPDRS,* 26th November 2007.

Mo Ibrahim Foundation (2008) *Rwanda the most improved country in Africa* {online}. Available online at: http://www.moibrahimfoundation.org/index-2008/pdf/press_release/Rwanda_English.pdf, accessed 13/07/09

Morgan, K. and Roberts, E. (2008): *The Democratic Deficit: A Guide to Quangoland*, Cardiff: Department of City and Regeneration Planning, University of Wales College of Cardiff.

Musoni, E. (2009) *Basic education program in crisis*, The New Times {online}, August 7th, 2009. Available at: http://www.newtimes.co.rw/index.php?issue=13980&article=18467 {accessed 07/0809}.

Musoni, E., and Kagire, E. (2009) *MPs Call for Stern Action on Ombudsman Report*, The New Times {online} July 9th, 2009. Available at:

http://www.newtimes.co.rw/index.php?issue=13951&article=17339 {accessed 09/07/09}.

Mutara, E. (2009) *City Businessman Arrested in Eastern Province Scam*, The New Times {online} May 2nd, 2009. Available online at: http://www.allafrica.com/stories/200905041394.html {accessed 05/08/09}.

Mutara, E. (2009) *Eastern Province Senior Official Arrested over Rw1.5 Billion*, The New Times {online} April 29th, 2009. Available at: http://www.allafrica.com/stories/200904290188.html {accessed 05/08/09}.

NCPPP (2008) *Open Letter to President-Elect Barack Obama* {online} dated 3rd 12, 2008, available at: http://www.ncppp.org/New%20Administration%20Ltr_0812.pdf {accessed 15/06/09}.

Nkubito, R. *(2009) The Journey Towards 2020,* The Sunday Times {online} June 7th, 2009. Available at: http://www.newtimes.co.rw/index.php?issue=13919&article=3903 {accessed 07/06/09}.

Obama, B. (2009) *Speech to Ghanaian Parliament*, Accra, July 11th, 2009.

Obore, C. (2009) *who is really behind the sale of Entebbe International Airport?* The Monitor {online} July 26th, 2009. Available at: http://www.monitor.co.ug/artman/publish/sun_news/who_is_really_behind_the_sale_of_Entebbe_International_Airport_88685.shtml {accessed 03/08/09}.

OECD (2008) *Public Private Partnerships: In Pursuit of Risk Sharing and Value for Money,* Paris: OECD.

OLPC (2009) *OLPC learning center opens in Kigali; Kagame presides over ceremony*, {online} June 11, 2009, available at: http://blog.laptop.org/2009/06/11/one-laptop-per-child-creates-a-global-center-for-excellence-in-laptops-and-learning {accessed 13/07/09}.

Osborne, S.P. ed., (2000) *Public-Private Partnerships: Theory and Practice in International Perspective*, London: Routledge

Pike, A. (2000) *The Private Sector and PPPs*, in Joseph, E. and Kelly, G. eds., (2000) *Finding the right partner: diversity in local public-private partnerships*. London: IPPR

Pollock, A., Price, D., Player, S. (2005) *The Private Finance Initiative: A Policy Built on Sand: an examination of the Treasury's evidence base for cost and time overrun data in value for money policy and appraisal*, London: Unison

Presidential Order N° 64/01 dated 31/12/2007, creating Rwanda Economic and Social Council (RESC)

Proving and Improving {n.d} *The ABCD Model: a quality and impact toolkit for social enterprise* [online}. Available at http://www.proveandimprove.org {accessed 09/06/09]

Redwood, J. (2004) *Public-Private Partnerships and Private Finance*, in Ghobadian, A., Gallear, D., O'Regan, N., and Viney, H., (eds.) (2004) *Public Private Partnerships: Policy and Experience*, Hampshire: Palgrave Macmillan

Republic of Rwanda (2009) *National Public Investment Policy*, adopted by the Cabinet on February 10, 2009. Kigali: GoR

Republic of Rwanda, Ministry of Finance and economic Planning (2007) *Rwanda Vision 2020* {Online}. Available at: http://www.minecofin.gov.rw [accessed 15/08/09}.

RESC (2009) *Minutes of Development Council Meeting*, May 22, 2009.

RISD (1999) *Land Use and Villagisation in Rwanda* {online} A Paper presented at the Land Use and Villagisation Workshop, Kigali, 20/21st September, 1999: Available at:http://www.oxfam.org.uk/resources/learning/landrights/downloads/risdsum mary.rtf {accessed 15/06/09}.

Rosenau, V. P. ed. (2000) *Public Private Policy Partnerships,* Massachusetts: The MIT Press.

Savas, E.S. (2000) *Privatization and Public-Private Partnerships*: New York: Seven Bridges Press LLC

Smith, A. (2007) *Risk management in Public Private Partnerships, value for money and the public sector comparator*, Farne Project Consultancy, Seoul, October2007 {online}. Available at:http://www.unescap.org/ttdw/ppp/PPP2007/risk_anthony_smith_bf.pdf [accessed 30/06/09}.

Smith, R. (2008) *Government Private Sector Partnerships as a Catalyst for Economic Growth and Development*, CPSU Conference on Corporate Social Responsibility, London, July 16th, 2008 {online}. Available at: http://www.cpsu.org.uk/fileadmin/Eco_Devt_and_Legal_Reform/Government_and_Private_sector_partnership_at_CSR_conference_RAINFORD_SMITH.doc {accessed 5/08/09}.

SOPHIE, C.N. (2005) *Union hits out at PFI waste* {online}. Available at http://www.cnplus.co.uk/news/union-hits-out-at-pfi-waste/616265.article accessed 16/06/09.

Stiem, T. (2009) *A new era dawns in Rwanda*, The Globe & Mail {online}, August 21, 2009. Available online at: http://www.theglobeandmail.com/life/travel/a-new-era-dawns-in-rwanda/article1259916/ {accessed 22/08/09}.

Taylor, M., Barr, A. & West, A. (2000) Signposts to Community Development, London: CDF

The National Audit Office report (2003b): *PFI Construction Performance* (Quoted in Gosling, 2004:35)

The Republic of Rwanda, The Ministry of Education (2006) *Strategic Plan* {online}. Available at: http://www.mineduc.gov.rw/spip.php?article20 {accessed 12/07/09}.

The World Bank (2006) *Youth in Community-Driven Development*, in Children & Youth, 1 (5) 1-4.

The World Bank Group (2008) *Private Participation in Infrastructure Database: PPI data update note19* (December 2008), Washington DC: The World Bank Group.

Tong-hyung. K. (2009) *KT Looks to Africa for Mobile Chance*, Korea Times {online} May 25th, 2009. Available at: http://www.koreatimes.co.kr/www/news/biz/2009/06/123_45659.html {accessed 22/ 06/09}.

Trochim, W.M.K. (2006) *The Philosophy of Research* {online} Web Center for

Social Research Methods. Available at http://www.socialresearchmethods.net {accessed 09/08/09].

UK DFID, (2007) *Free Education Means a Future for Rwanda's Children,* {online}, DFID Publication of 15 October 2007. Available at: http://www.dfid.gov.uk/casestudies/files/africa/rwanda-schools.asp {accessed 25/11/08}.

UNDP (20004) *Public Partnerships for Urban Environment: Tools for pro-people municipal PPP* {online}: Available at: http://www.margrafpublishers.com/UNDP/PPPUE/MOD013.htm {accessed 09/07/09}.

UNDP Rwanda, *Vacancy Announcement*, 26 March 2009.

University of York (2006) *Code of Good Practice for Research* {online}. Available at: http://www.york.ac.uk/research/policy/code_of_practice_research.htm#4_Ethics {accessed 09/082009}.

US Department of Transportation, Federal Highway Administration guidelines on PPP, available at http://www.fhwa.dot.gov/ppp, accessed 23rd, 2009

US Department of Transportation, Federal Highway Administration {online}. Available at http://www.fhwa.dot.gov/reports/pppwave/03.htm {accessed 15/06/09].

US GAO (2008) *Highway Public-Private Partnerships: Securing Potential Benefits and Protecting the Public Interest Could Result from More Rigorous Up-front Analysis,* Statement of JayEtta Z. Hecker, Director physical Infrastructure Issues, to the U.S Senate, July 24, 2008, Washington DC:

United States Government Accountability Office

Woo-Cumings, M., ed. (1999) *The Developmental State,* New York: Cornell University Press

World Bank Institute (2006) *Initiating a Global Network of Public-Private Partnership for Infrastructure* {online}. Available at: http://web.worldbank.org/WBSITE/EXTERNAL/TOPICS/EXTCDRC/0,,contentMDK:21005958~menuPK:64169181~pagePK:64169212~piPK:64169110~theSitePK:489952,00.html {accessed 13/08/09}.

Yin, R.K. (2003) *Case Study Research: Design and Methods* (3rd edn.) Thousand Oaks, Ca: Sage Publications

Appendices:

Appendix A: Explanatory Statement and Consent Form

Dissertation research project. Summer 2009.

Ignatius Mugabo

timuga73@hotmail.com

M: 07973787229

What Impact has Public-Private Partnership had on Community Development in Rwanda?
A Case Study of Education Sector 1994-1998

Explanatory Statement:

I am currently enrolled on the *Organisation and Community Development* Masters programme at the London Metropolitan University in the United Kingdom. A Dissertation research forms a core component of this course. My research centres on the Public-Private Partnership (PPP) policy in Rwanda and how it can contribute to community development.

I am interested in this policy area because it's increasingly becoming an important concept in public sector management and infrastructure development, and I think it marries well the interest of both the public and private sectors. Rwanda is one of the countries in Africa that are taking on this concept to provide infrastructure development in the country. Being Rwandan I am naturally interested in whatever is happening in Rwanda.

My line of enquiry is: what consideration, if any the PPP policy in Rwanda gives to community development? If it is not considered, why not and what contribution to community development could it make? What is the relationship between community development and economic development? I will examine and analyse some PPP case studies in the education sector and make recommendations informed by the good practice and standards for community development practice.

This research will rely heavily on literature review and analysis of relevant policy documents, but I am also very keen to interview some Rwandan officials or international organizations officials who have been involved in development/economic policy in Rwanda.

In the interest of good research practice and in keeping with applicable University ethical codes and guidelines, a set of criteria has been devised:

a) All participants must be over the age of 18. No, children, minors or vulnerable people are allowed to take part in this research

b) The research being conducted is purely for my dissertation and any data collected shall not be used for anything else

c) There are no anticipated risks to participants and no remuneration
d) Participants will give their consent freely and can withdraw consent at any time without any penalty
e) All discussions will be completely anonymous and details will never be shared with any other participant or organisation
f) Confidentiality shall be guaranteed to all participants

Any questions or queries can be directed to me using the contacts at the top of the page.

Thanking you in advance for your kind cooperation

Ignatius Mugabo

Masters in Organisation and Community Development Student

Dissertation research project. Summer 2009.

Ignatius Mugabo

timuga73@hotmail.com

M: 07973787229

What Impact has Public-Private Partnership had on Community Development in Rwanda?

A Case Study of Education Sector 1994-2008

Consent

I agree to take part in the above MSc. Dissertation research project interview. I have had the project explained to me, and I have a copy of the Explanatory Statement, which I may keep for my records. I understand that agreeing to take part means that I'm willing to:

a) be interviewed by the researcher

b) have the interview recorded

c) Be identified – YES/NO (please delete as appropriate)

I'm over the age of 18 years of age and am willing to contribute my ideas freely.

I understand that the information I provide is confidential, and no information I give which could lead to my identification unless I agree to be identified, or that of those I may speak about, will be disclosed in any reports on the project or to any other party.

No identifiable data will be published, nor be shared with any other organisation.

Name...Position................................

Signature............................Date.................................

Appendix B: Former Military College, now KIST
(Images used with the kind permission of the Rector of KIST)

Appendix C: Abbreviations and Acronyms

ABCD	Achieving Better Community Development
AfDB	African Development Bank
BBO	Buy-Build-Operate
BOO	Build-Own-Operate
BOOT	Build-Own-Operate-Transfer
CCPPP	Canadian Council for Public Private Partnerships
CD	Community Development
CDD	Community Driven Development
CDF	Community Development Foundation
CDF	Community Development Fund
CHRI	Commonwealth Human Rights Initiative
CITT	Centre for Innovation and Technology Transfer
CNN	Cable News Network
CPSU	Commonwealth Policy Studies Unit
DASS	Department for Applied Social Sciences
DB	Design-Build
DBFO	Design-Build-Finance-and-Operate
DFID	Department for International Development
DOT	Department of Transportation (USA)
EAC	East African Community
EC	European Commission
EDPRS	Economic Development & Poverty Reduction Strategy
EIB	European Investment Bank
EoR	Embassy of Rwanda
ESRC	Economic and Social Research Council
EU	European Union
FHWA	Federal Highway Administration (USA)
GAO	Government Accountability Office (USA)
GoR	Government of Rwanda
HMSO	Her Majesty's Stationery Office
GTZ	German Agency for Technical Co-operation
IMF	International Monetary Fund

	IPPR	Institute of Public Policy Research
	KDS	Korea Institute for Development Strategy
	KIST	Kigali Institute of Science and Technology
	KOICA	Korea International Co-operation Agency
	KT	Korea Telecom
	LDO	Lease-Develop-Operate
	LFB	London Fire Brigade
	LFEPA	London Fire and Emergency Planning Authority
	LMBS	London Metropolitan Business School
	MDGs	Millennium Development Goals
MINALOC		Ministry of Local Government
MINECOFIN		Ministry of Finance & Economic Planning
MINEDUC		Ministry of Education
	MNCs	Multinational Corporations
	NAO	National Audit Office
	NCDC	National Curriculum Development Centre
	NCPPP	National Council for Public Private Partnerships
	NCHE	National Council for Higher Education
	NEPAD	New Partnership for Africa's Development
	NHS	National Health Service
	NOS	National Occupation Standards (for community development)
	OLF	Open Learning Foundation
	O&M	Operation & Maintenance
	OECD	Organization for Economic Co-operation and Development
	OLPC	One Laptop per Child
	OSR&D	Office of Scientific Research & Development
	PFI	Private Finance Initiative
	NPIP	National Public Investment Policy
	PITT	Public Investment Technical Team
	PPP	Public Private Partnership
	PPPUE	Public Private Partnership for Urban Environment
	PSC	Public Sector Comparator
	PSF	Private Sector Federation (of Rwanda)
	RESC	Rwanda Economic and Social Council
	R&D	Research & Development

RDB	Rwanda Development Board
REC	Research Ethics Committee
RISD	Rwanda Integrated & Sustainable Development
S&P	Standard & Poor's
SFAR	Students Financing Agency of Rwanda
TSC	Teachers' Service Commission
UK	United Kingdom (of Great Britain and Northern Ireland)
UKTI	United Kingdom Trade & Investment
UNDP	United Nations Development Programme
UNECA	United Nations Economic Commission for Africa
UNECE	United Nations Economic Commission for Europe
UNESCO	United Nations Education Scientific and Cultural Organization
USA	United States of America
VfM	Value for Money
WB	World Bank

VDM publishing house ltd.

Scientific Publishing House
offers
free of charge publication

of current academic research papers, Bachelor´s Theses, Master's Theses, Dissertations or Scientific Monographs

If you have written a thesis which satisfies high content as well as formal demands, and you are interested in a remunerated publication of your work, please send an e-mail with some initial information about yourself and your work to *info@vdm-publishing-house.com*.

Our editorial office will get in touch with you shortly.

VDM Publishing House Ltd.
Meldrum Court 17.
Beau Bassin
Mauritius
www.vdm-publishing-house.com

Printed in Great Britain
by Amazon.co.uk, Ltd.,
Marston Gate.